Skunk Tales

Making Sense of Scents

SKUNK TALES
MAKING SENSE OF SCENTS

Lynn Marie Hurtado

A Family Devotional

Skunk Tales
by Lynn Marie Hurtado
ISBN: 978-0-9826363-0-5
Subject Heading: Family Devotional

Published in the United States of America by:
New Lineage
P.O. Box 293892
Kerrville, TX 78029
skunktalesonline.com

Final layout, typesetting, and editing done by Brandon Ashton.
brandon.ashton.books@gmail.com

Printed in the United States of America.

"The earth is the Lord's and everything in it..." Psalm 24:1

Dedicated to the honor and glory of my Lord and Savior, Jesus Christ.

In memory of my Father, Thomas Bernard, whose
words of blessing still encourage me today.

In memory of my Mother, Betty Jane, whose words of
wisdom have taught me many valuable lessons.

With love to my son, Alex, for the joy these remembrances
bring in reminding me how blessed my life is.

With all my heart, I thank my Heavenly Father who has been unspeakably gracious to me by preserving the vivid memories and details of each story in this book.

From inspiration to publication, my loving appreciation goes to the following people:

Brandon Ashton, Richard Holcomb, Kyung Won Lee, Patty May, Susan McGinnis, Sany Nathanson, Barbara Neidnagel, Suzanne Stinson, Brad and JooYoung Voeller, Ryan and Julianne Yamane, Child Evangelism Fellowship, Circle Christian School, First Baptist Church of Orlando, Orlando Grace Church, Texas Parks and Wildlife Department.

Special recognition for the folks of the Moses Lake community where the majority of these Skunk Tales were written. Their hospitality and many kindnesses extended to me during my stay there are unsurpassed.

With gratitude to my son Alex who first had the vision for Pooky's Time Out.

Heartfelt thanks to the artists:

Ruthann J Keulen
Chapter illustrations

Emily Schultz
Cover art and preface page illustrations

Timothy Ray Sprunger
"Pooky's Time Out" icon

Table of Contents

*"For we did not follow cleverly devised tales
when we made known to you the power
and coming of our Lord Jesus Christ, but
we were eyewitnesses of His majesty."*

2 PETER 1:16 (NASB)

Foreword

Have you ever wondered why God trusts us with children before He entrusts us with the wisdom to raise them? There is no greater affirmation of how it is "God at work in you" than this impossible task of parenting to "bring children up in the nurture and admonition of the Lord." In other words, we are intended to learn by doing!

It also underscores how much we need and benefit from other "apprentice parents" who have taken seriously the clear assignment of "talking of these things (God's Word) when you sit in your house, walk by the way, rise up, and lie down" (Deuteronomy 6:6–7).

Such a parent is Lynn Marie Hurtado. I have known her since she was just starting on this gospel road over twenty years ago and have marveled at how the repeated difficulties and impossibilities of a single mom raising a son alone can accomplish so much by simple and resolute faith in the Scripture's sufficiency. It consistently resulted in persevering grace and wisdom to "prove the good, acceptable, and perfect will of God" and to prepare the next generation to do the same. Here is a collection of stories of a parent like you who wants her descendants to "set their hope in God and not forget the works of God...but set their hearts aright" (Psalm 78:5–8) by simple, daily attempts at talking of God's Word. St. Augustine would call this "using this world to love God more."

You and all your little "assignments" will benefit from her example. You are writing a book, too. Your children are your epistle, the epistle of Christ Himself, and you have the privilege of co-authoring this epistle on their hearts (2 Corinthians 3:2–3).

–Timothy Pent

About This Book

This book was written to inspire and encourage families with true, original stories from the different chapters of my life. My desire is for families like yours to enjoy reading these exciting, firsthand testimonies while learning how to recognize the little lessons that God is teaching you daily. As you continue to teach Christian values to your growing family, Skunk Tales will challenge you and your children to turn the untold experiences from your lives into faith-building lessons that you will always remember.

In the year 2002 my son Alex and I lived and worked at a retreat center in the Hill Country area outside of San Antonio, Texas. Living in the country was a challenging and harrowing experience for a family like ours who had lived in a big city. With the abundant wildlife there in the country we were often confronted with opportunities to parallel our life lessons with the habits and indulgences of the wild animals. In God's providence, these day-in and day-out occurences lent to the writing of these experiences.

During the four years we lived at the retreat center we strangely had more encounters with skunks than the normal household. The inquisitive animals showed up at our home on a somewhat continual basis. Moving from the camp was not a possibility at the time and the skunks were not going to leave. After all, they were wild animals. After one particularly stressful day of concern about the skunks, I called a girlfriend to express my ongoing frustration and discontentment. "Is this another skunk tale?" she asked. She always encouraged me to hold fast to my faith no matter what and scolded me for worrying about the smelly critters. The story "Bench Press" is where the quote first appears that became the title of the book.

It was at that time I began to pull together notes and entrees from my journals of the miraculous ways that God had been with us from the beginning, through all the circumstances of our lives. Those written lines had preserved well the memories of the daily communion with my Heavenly Father and how He heard the outcries and prayers of a mother and her son. Prayers from when I was a little girl that were answered. The stories reveal the day-by-day childlike faith between a loving Father and our young family. Our theology was the Bible, prayer, and God.

Through the next thirty-six chapters, you will laugh and cry with Alex and me as we learn lessons from our encounters with animals of all different shapes, sizes, and scents. The first two chapters take place when we arrive at the retreat center. The next few chapters flash back to my childhood where I share stories about my family. The remaining stories tell about memories I made with Alex throughout his childhood as we homeschooled together and encouraged each other in the Lord.

Follow the small paw prints in the shaded box at the end of each chapter, and you will discover a fun animal fact, scripture reference, or trivia. Last, but not least, at the end of each chapter you will find Pooky's Time . Out which I hope will become a familiar delight to you. Alex thought that it would be a good idea to have a time of reflection or "time out" after each story and specifically challenge children. There are an array of activities to choose from that pertain in some way to each tale. The worship songs for each chapter were chosen to help you remember the meaning of the stories. You will benefit and enjoy the practical hands-on activities in Pooky's Time Out that have been inspired by the true events in the stories.

These incidents may be unique to me as I tell about them from my point of view, but they are common occurrences to those who live in and about the country where skunks are most commonly found. Today I appreciate how God made skunks so unique, and I can be grateful as I look back at all that I have learned from them. These Skunk Tales highlight the experiences that have taught me what is most important in life.

I invite you to join me and share in these light-hearted yet life-giving adventures. You will benefit from these true examples and glean a fresh perspective of the unchangeable circumstances of life. Learn how God can triumphantly take you from scents to sense. It has been a joy writing these tales for you. I hope you enjoy the stories.

Chapter 1

Tap Dance

"I lie down and sleep; I wake again,
because the LORD sustains me."

PSALM 3:5

Our family had recently moved from the beautiful Sunshine State of Florida to the wide open spaces of Texas. The unknowns and uncertainties before us felt as big and wide as the state itself. We were volunteers at the retreat center where we were staying while searching for a place to live. Growing more impatient, I wondered when the day would come that we would know where our home would be.

One summer night, decisions and thoughts about the future began to interfere with my sleep. Alex heard me stirring and got out of bed to see what I was doing.

"Mom, why are you still up? It's late."

"I thought I'd read for awhile. I can't sleep," I answered. Thinking about a place to live was keeping me up at night. I imagined the possibilities of what life would be like living in the country. The next day was going to be busy at the retreat center with lawn work and gardening. We needed our rest but I tossed and turned until the morning.

"How are you feeling this morning, Mom?" Alex asked the next day as he walked by me, pushing a wheelbarrow full of plants.

"Oh, I'm still daydreaming about where we're going to live," I said hazily as I pulled weeds in the flowerbeds. I was fatigued from lack of sleep and was having a difficult time being cheerful. The Texas heat was getting to my head, and my burdens were weighing down my heart.

Silently I prayed. *Lord, please help me rest in you today.* Carefully pacing myself, I made a special effort to avoid exhaustion. The long, hot day felt like a week. Placing each plant delicately in the earth, I patted the warm soil around it. By the end of the day I was tired and ready to give a night's rest another try.

"I'm glad for this day to be over," I told Alex, regretting I was not more enthusiastic. It was a welcomed relief to go back to our quaint, comfortable room. The thought of turning off the lights and getting into bed never seemed so good. The country was extremely quiet at night; you could *hear a pin drop.*

When I lay down to rest, I could hear my heart beating. I thought I would fall fast asleep, but this was not the case. Thoughts of the day paraded through my mind. *God, help me to trust you with our destination,* I prayed.

Turning over in bed, I thought I heard a noise in the wall down near the floor. *It must be my imagination,* I first thought, *or maybe I've had too much sun.* The next noise was followed by a scratch, and then the scratch got a little louder. It crept closer to me, just inside the wall. Rolling over on my back, I stared up into the pitch-dark ceiling. *What can it be?*

I quietly woke up Alex. "There's a noise in the wall. Please come check it out." He came into my room and pressed his ear against the wall. The scratching had stopped.

"Mom, are you sure you heard something?" he asked.

"Yes, I'm sure, but now it's gone," I whispered. "Maybe it was a little mouse or a friendly rat. You can go back to bed now, Son. It's alright."

Once again, my mind began to drift and wander, thinking about where we would be moving. The distraction became worry, and now I was not fully resting in the Lord. Saying yet another prayer, I asked God to help me trust Him as I tried to fall asleep.

The scratching began again and slowly moved its way through the wall until it was directly behind the headboard. It stopped for a few seconds and then started up again. This went on for some time. I wondered what it could be, but more than that, how I could stop it. *Should I wake up Alex?* I thought to myself. There was nothing he could do about it tonight, I decided.

The scratching sounded like the sawing of a logger. I sat up in bed and knocked softly on the wall with my hand. The noise stopped for a few seconds. Relieved, I thought the little critter had fled. Well, yes he fled, but to the other side of the bed, and this time his scratching was louder and longer.

With a pencil I snatched from my nightstand, I started tapping on the wall, hoping to shoo away whatever it was. I tapped, he halted. When I stopped tapping, he started scratching again. It sounded like something was scraping, building, or nesting right inside the wall. We were doing a tap dance!

Lying back down in bed listening to the noises gave me lots of time to think and pray. Reflecting on the last few days, I realized that I had not trusted the Lord for all our needs. What could I do? I could not do anything about my noisy, uninvited guest, and I could not settle tonight where we would be living. Where was my cheerful, patient spirit?

That tap-dancer kept me awake all night. The scratching in the wall became a tugging in my heart. I knew I could not remove the critter that night; what I could do was remove my bad attitudes and choose to trust the Lord. Exhausted, I knelt down beside my bed and prayed thanking God for cleansing my heart of ungratefulness, impatience, and worry. Finally, my heart and mind were free!

Rising from my bedside, I walked out onto the balcony. Dawn was breaking, and the morning sun peeked over the Texas horizon. Alex soon joined me to welcome the new day.

"Good morning, Mom. How did you sleep?"

Smiling, I replied, "Oh, I didn't sleep, Son. I worked all night."

"Work! What work did you do in the middle of the night?" he asked with a smile.

"Let's just say that I stayed up to take care of business—business with the Lord, that is!"

Just then, an opossum ran out from under the house and scurried across the grass.

"There's my tap-dancing partner, Alex. I guess he's finished with his business, too!" And he was.

Opossums are marsupials which are unique because they carry their young in a pouch on their bellies. They have very sharp claws and more than fifty teeth. When confronted by a predator an opossum will play dead as a defense until danger passes. Opossums hide in hollowed trees, attics and roofs. They are primarily nocturnal.

Discussion

What is your favorite bedtime routine? What do you do when you cannot fall asleep? What is the difference between caring and worrying? What cares do you have to bring to the Lord? How can a cheerful attitude make our hearts glad?

Scripture

"I will praise the LORD, who counsels me; even at night my heart instructs me." Psalm 16:7

"A cheerful heart is good medicine, but a crushed spirit dries up the bones." Proverbs 17:22

"Come to me, all you who are weary and burdened, and I will give you rest." Matthew 11:28

"Cast all your anxiety on him because he cares for you." 1 Peter 5:7

Song

"I Must Tell Jesus" and "Cast All My Cares Upon You"

Activity

Gather around a table. Tap and hum your favorite tune while everyone tries to guess what tune it is. The one who guesses first goes next.

Application

On those sleepless nights, choose a scripture and memorize (for example, Psalm 3:5). Take turns reading your favorite bedtime stories to your siblings. Write a personal family prayer and memorize to recite at bedtime. Spend some time counting your blessings before you go to sleep, and record them in a gratitude journal.

Idiom

Hear a pin drop means it is so quiet you can hear very faint things.

Prayer

Thank the Lord for watching over you while you sleep. Be sure to cast your cares upon Him.

Chapter 2

Line in the Sand

*"The boundary lines have fallen for me in pleasant
places; surely I have a delightful inheritance."*

PSALM 16:6

We had been looking for a place to move when we called our pastor to meet with him. Moving was no small thing, and I was hoping that he could give us some direction and encouragement.

"Let's pray and wait. The Lord will direct you," he advised. Our pastor was a faithful man of prayer. After our meeting, he walked us out to our car. He then did something that was unexpected. He picked up a stick from the ground, knelt in the sand, and drew a map in the shape of our city, a simple line map.

"Here's our city," he said. He drew a line near the center of the city and pointed to the middle of the line. "This would be a good place for you to live. It's a great neighborhood and a convenient location for you." He was familiar with the area, and it was close to some families we already knew. We stood there and prayed.

The following month, to our surprise, the "line in the sand" became reality. The retreat center where we had been staying was exactly where he had pointed. After volunteering for several weeks at the camp, our family was offered a staff position and a place to live. God had generously and miraculously answered our prayers, and this ministry center would be our new home.

We were excited to move out of our one room into a house at the camp. We had dreamed of living in the country with the fresh air and open space. We drove up to our new front yard, pulling the small trailer filled with all of our possessions. We were anxious to unload the trailer and get settled into our new place.

"Welcome to the neighborhood," said a pretty lady who was waiting for us with a basket of goodies. After a few minutes of friendly conversation, we were all chased indoors by a sudden cloudburst. Our unpacking was delayed, but we were glad to have a roof over us and a new friend.

After the rain stopped, we were unloading and stacking the boxes in the living room while leaving muddy footprints on the floor. The boxes seemed to have a musty odor to them. *Could some of them have gotten wet?* I wondered. Alex walked into the other room; I thought he went to get something from the basket of treats.

"Do you smell something strange, Alex?" I called out.

"Yes, it smells like Cheetos in here," he answered.

We looked around the house to see if we could find what was producing the foul smell. *Could it be a dead mouse under the kitchen sink?* I took a look, and did not find a thing.

"Alex, would you check the closets for mildew?"

"Mom, I don't see any," he reported back.

It was getting dark when Alex ran outside to find the source of the smell. He disappeared into the dusky brush. I watched from the back porch wondering what he might find and dreading what the smell could be. Feeling distracted from my moving duties, I went back inside to unpack some things we might need for the night.

A short time later, I heard shuffling at the back door, the sound of someone kicking mud from their boots. It was Alex coming back into the house with a grimace on his face.

"Mom, I have to prepare you for something," he announced.

"I don't like to have to tell you this, but I think we have a skunk!"

"A skunk! What makes you think it's a skunk?"

"The stinky smell is even stronger outside," he explained.

"What do you mean it's stronger?" I desperately asked.

"Well, Mom, it's like this—rain plus stunk, equals skunk!" he rhymed with a wince. The damp ground had turned the strong odor into a vapor of smelly, stale stench.

I opened the front door, and sure enough, the knee-weakening stink nearly knocked us off our feet. I closed the door quickly and looked around the room full of boxes, collapsing on the sturdiest one I could find. A wave of gloom slowly overcame me. Our new house was surrounded by an annoying, menacing, stinky skunk trail. I sat down to *collect myself*. This was the last thing I ever expected to happen when we moved.

"Come on, Alex. Let's go sit in the car and watch for a skunk." That seemed like the next best thing to do. What would we do if we found one?

We tip-toed through the wet grass to the car, and our muddy boots were now tainted with traces of the foul, mysterious odor. Sitting in the car with the windows cracked opened, the rain trickled down once again. With flashlights in hand, we sat watching for even the slightest movement. The only action, however, was the neighbor's cat eating on their front porch. Several hours had passed, and the panic left us as the weariness of the day settled upon us.

We went back into the house, cold, damp, and stiff-necked from the futile evening watch. We still did not know the identity of the mysterious smell. The first night in our new house was the beginning of a journey that we would not have been able to imagine on our own.

"Well, we know the Lord lead us here," I assured Alex. We remembered the day we prayed with our pastor, and we were confident that our new home was the answer to that prayer. The line in the sand symbolized an unknown future and trust in the providence of God.

What unforeseen adventures awaited us? What was that smell, and where was it coming from? Would we ever know? Would we trust God through these smelly circumstances? With His help we did. The mystery was solved in the weeks ahead, but that is another story.

> *Skunks belong to the family* Mephitidae *which is derived from the Latin word for "stink." Because a skunk cannot outrun a predator, it relies on its scent glands for protection. Skunk odor is called musk. Skunk musk is called "nature's tear gas." The smell can travel for several miles depending on wind and weather. Rain will revive old skunk odor.*

Discussion

What does it means to trust someone? Can you give one example of how your parent or pastor cares for you? What is something for which you are trusting God? Discuss that sometimes we do not know where God is leading, but that we can always trust Him.

Scripture

"Those who know your name will trust in you, for you, LORD, have never forsaken those who seek you." Psalm 9:10

"Trust in the LORD with all your heart and lean not on your own understanding; in all your ways acknowledge him, and he will make your paths straight." Proverbs 3:5–6

"Do not let your hearts be troubled. Trust in God; trust also in me." John 14:1

Song

"Great Is Thy Faithfulness" and "Day By Day".

Activity

Write your own lyrics to the tune "A-Hunting We Will Go" using different animal names. March and sing along. For example,

> We'll catch a skunk, and stick him in the trunk,
> (Chorus) Heigh-ho, the dairy-o, and then we'll let him go.
> We'll catch a fox, and keep him in a box... (Chorus)
> We'll catch a dog, and tie him to a log... (Chorus)

Application

Trust Walk: Draw a line outside in the sand. Blindfold your child, and have him walk toward you on the line trusting you for safety as you whisper directions. Cheer him on.

Idiom

Collect myself means to take time to calm down.

Prayer

Trust the Lord to help you with any uncertainties you may have.

Chapter 3

Ribbon Candy

"Jesus said, 'Let the little children come to me, and do not hinder them, for the kingdom of heaven belongs to such as these.'"

MATTHEW 19:14

Signs were posted throughout the neighborhood announcing the upcoming Backyard Bible School at the project where I lived. I had never been to a Bible School of any kind, so I could not imagine what to expect. It was Saturday, and the day we were awaiting had finally arrived.

> · BACKYARD BIBLE SCHOOL
> · REFRESHMENTS
> THIS SATURDAY

"Mama, it's time for the Bible School. Can we go now?"

"Yes, Lynn Marie, and watch out for your sister," Mother said as she hugged us good-bye. My little sister Debbie and I jumped on our bicycles and rode to the courtyard with Sandy, an older neighbor girl who accompanied us. Florida's long, hot summer days made us glad it was early morning. All along the sidewalk on our way, children of all ages streamed to the open square where the Bible School was to be held. We could not wait to see what had everyone so excited.

As we approached, I saw a block of metal poles in the center of the square. They looked like an old set of monkey bars from an abandoned playground. Children were jumping and playing on the poles, waiting for the event to begin.

When we got closer, we saw a little, grey-haired lady calling, "Come children, come now, let's sit down." Children scurried from all corners of the yard to find a place on the spotty grass. Debbie and I were shy, so we made our way to the back of the group.

She was a sweet little lady, the one who came to teach the Bible study that day. I do not recall her name, just how kind she was. She wore a yellow blouse with a big white button. She pulled out a wooden easel and a blue felt board and set them in front for all to see.

"I am so happy to be here with you today," she said with joy beaming from her face. "How many of you have ever been to a Backyard Bible School?" Only a few raised their hands. All the little faces were looking straight ahead when the teacher instructed us to bow our heads as she said a short prayer.

"Dear Jesus, thank you for this day. Please bless our time together. I pray that the seeds planted here today will bring forth much fruit. In Jesus' name, Amen."

The teacher told us the story about how Jesus took something small and used it to bless many people. It was the story about a boy with five barley loaves and two fishes. "God used the boy's small amount of food to bless many others," the teacher explained. "We all have something we can give."

I looked intently as the sweet lady placed a paper figure of Jesus on the blue felt board along with a figure of a boy, five loaves of bread, and two fishes.

"Jesus gave thanks and then broke the bread. The boy showed he was thankful by sharing with others. Jesus multiplied the boy's food and passed it around to thousands of hungry people who had come to hear him speak." The teacher continued, "The boy in the story sacrificed by giving what he had, yet he still had enough for himself." The children sat still and quietly listened.

When the story was finished, we sang a song. "Jesus loves me, this I know, for the Bible tells me so. Yes, Jesus loves me!"

"That's right, children. Jesus loves you!" said the teacher. The words stayed in my mind all day.

The kind teacher took the board and the paper figures and put them away in a box. The children were getting antsy, and the quiet time was about to end. The teacher had her back to the group for just a few seconds. Slowly, she turned around with a big smile on her face. She was holding a colorful tin canister.

"There is one more thing I would like to share with you before we go," she announced. *What could that be?* I thought. It looked like a container of marbles, maybe, or bubble gum. She summoned us to come forward and form a line.

I rushed to get in line as quickly as I could trying to get a closer peek. I could not see very well, but one by one, the other children returned with a big hard piece of bright, swirly ribbon candy.

"Look at that, Sissy, we get a piece of candy!" I told Debbie.

Yummy, does that look good, I thought. I was so excited. I had never seen anything like that before. The candy was twisted, colorful, and pretty. I was all smiles by the time I reached the front of the line. As I held my hand out, I said, "Thank you. This looks so good!"

We rushed home with a skip, savoring each lick of the sweet, beautiful ribbon candy. "Mommy, look at this candy. It's so pretty!" Debbie said, dashing to the door. My sister and I raced to tell Mother all about the Backyard Bible School.

"Mommy, it was so much fun! My favorite part was the ribbon candy," I said, licking the sticky, striped, delight.

"Someone was faithful to buy that ribbon candy for the Bible School. They were thinking of others," Mother said.

"Just like the boy with the loaves of bread and the fishes," I told her, reciting what I could remember from the story that day.

"Someone cared enough to think of a small thing like candy, so that you would be blessed. And the sweet Bible teacher was faithful to come and teach you today," Mother pointed out to us, and she was right.

That day at the courtyard changed my life forever. God used small acts of kindness in a very big way. The Lord used that faithful lady that I did not know to sow seeds of God's Word into my heart. I went to the Backyard Bible School every Saturday that summer to hear the Bible stories and to enjoy some sweet treats.

The kind teacher continued teaching the Bible in my neighborhood for many years. Her *labor of love* for the Lord Jesus planted seeds of faith into the lives of countless children. Years later, my Mother would still buy me colorful tin cans of ribbon candy in remembrance of those Backyard Bible School days. She knew it meant so much to me. Small things do matter.

"We continually remember before our God and Father your work produced by faith, your labor prompted by love, and your endurance inspired by hope in our Lord Jesus Christ." 1 Thessalonians 1:3

Discussion

How did the Bible teacher show faithfulness to God? How does God show His faithfulness to you everyday? Who shared the Good News (Gospel) with you? What do you have that you could share? Parents, what blessings do you enjoy today because someone in your past was faithful ?

From the Bible

"At that time Jesus said, "I praise you, Father, Lord of heaven and earth, because you have hidden these things from the wise and learned, and revealed them to little children." Matthew 11:25

"His master replied, 'Well done, good and faithful servant! You have been faithful with a few things; I will put you in charge of many things. Come and share your master's happiness!" Matthew 25:21

"Jesus then took the loaves, gave thanks, and distributed to those who were seated as much as they wanted. He did the same with the fish." John 6:11

Song

"Jesus Loves Me" and "Tell Me The Story Of Jesus"

Application

Bake a sweet treat. Share it with someone to bless them. Show genuine interest in them as a person created in the image of God. Celebrate the "Good News" with someone close to you. Reminisce over photos of family members or friends who in some way contributed to your Christian heritage. Send a note of thanks to that special someone who has encouraged you in your faith.

Idiom

Labor of love means a special act done for love, not for personal gain.

Prayer

Praise the Lord for the faithful servant who brought you the Good News.

Chapter 4

Dippy Dell

"You open your hand and satisfy the
desires of every living thing."

PSALM 145:16

"Okay, Debbie, let's get our room cleaned so we can go down to the creek." I was the older sister, so I got to check the chores. "Come and help me get this stuff out from under the bed," I told her as I pushed the clutter out with a broom.

"Oh, you mean under the bed counts, too? I thought I was all finished," she said, not knowing that I knew better.

Mother, who was keeping a close ear to our conversations in the nearby room making sure that my instructions were kind, called, "Yes, Dippy Dell. I want it *spic-and-span* under that bed."

"And let's put your 'babies' away in the closet, too." I told her. After I inspected our room, I took Debbie by the hand and led her to Mother. "Come on, Sissy, let Mommy fix your pigtails, and then we can go out to play."

Debbie and I did everything together. The creek by our house was one of our favorite places to go. "I'll get the bucket and net. Let's go," said Debbie as she hurried to the door.

"Bye, Mama. We'll be back in a little while," I said, glancing at Mother to see if she had any objections.

"Be careful, and remember, only dip your toes! I'll be on the back porch watching, and bring home some good loot, too" After a little hug and squeeze from Mother, we ran out, the screen door slamming behind us. We were never out of Mother's sight. Barefoot and carefree, we could now embark on our favorite weekend ritual—pursuit of wild loot!

"You go over there, and I'll stand here on this branch," Debbie said as she took command of our positions on the creek's edge. She usually liked to stand in the same prominent place. Old roots resembling branches ran down into the water from the surrounding trees. Debbie liked to get near the edge, just close enough to wet her toes. This was as far as we could go, even though it was not deep. "NEVER SWIM ALONE," Mother always reminded us. This is just one of the safety rules you have to follow in Florida, when you live near the water.

"Oh, the water is so cold," Debbie said as she eased her toes into the stream. Looking back over her shoulder, she checked to be sure Mother was still nearby. She was sitting on the back porch, faithfully looking our way. Debbie loved to dip her toes in the water and then quickly pull them out. Her middle name was Dell, so that is why we called her "Dippy Dell."

We staked out close to the edge of the water for a specific reason. Debbie had a favorite pet that she liked to catch and play with. We were on the lookout for Little Grass Frogs. We could hear their high-pitched voice, it sounded like the tinkle of glass. They were hard to spot because they were less than an inch long. Their chocolate-brown, baby-soft skin blended in with the dark, muddy bank of the creek. We usually found them perched on the broken roots and branches just above the surface of the water, perfect spots for Debbie to bend down and scoop them up. Even though she had a little net, she just loved to catch them with her hands and stroke their silky skin.

"Oh, look how cute he is," she cooed as she patted one on its little back. "Where are his Mother and Father?" she asked. "They might get lost downstream," she explained as she picked up more little frogs and held them close to her chest, snuggling them before she placed them in the bucket.

"What are you going to do with them all, Debbie?" I always asked this same question, and she always gave the same answer.

"I'm going to give them a home; they need a Mommy," she would reply. Standing near the waters edge, I watched for frogs to jump into sight so Debbie could move in and scoop them up.

"There they are, there they are—get 'em!" I cried, and we scrambled for the prize loot. We hopped about around the creek's edge, snatching up as many tiny frogs as we could.

"How many frogs do we have now?" I asked.

"It's hard to count them. They won't sit still, but I think we have eleven, twelve, or maybe even thirteen," Debbie said trying to count each one. The frogs were jumping up the sides of the plastic bucket trying to escape. Mother was now standing to her feet, a sign that it was time for our outdoor adventure to end.

"Come home now. It's time to come in," she waved with a smile. We gathered our things and ran home. Dippy Dell had a bucket full of joy.

"Good girls, you were obedient. I saw you only got your toes wet. How was your catch today? Did you bring home some loot?" Mother considered everything we did important and called anything that was meaningful to us "loot."

Mother and I stood and watched Dippy Dell dump the bucket over into the grass so that we could count how many frogs she had caught. Like little frogs do, they jumped in every direction.

"Oh no, don't let them get away!" Debbie cried. We frantically tried to catch the little frogs, but they slipped right through our hands. We watched them surface above the grass and disappear again as they made their way back home to the creek.

"There go my little baby frogs," Debbie sadly said. "I wanted to keep them for my very own."

Mother gently pulled her close and said, "Those little frogs have their own home, and they want to be with their own Mommy."

Debbie whimpered, "I want to be a Mommy when I grow up."

"You'll be a good Mommy one day," Mother softly said. Our Mother always knew how to comfort us.

Dippy Dell never turned away an opportunity to pet and nurture any animal that she came across. She has had eleven dogs and seven cats throughout her life. She has had a natural desire in her heart to love and care for others and to be a Mother one day. My sister Debbie had two children of her own. A Mother's love demonstrates God's love for His children.

The Little Grass Frog is the smallest frog in North America. This small amphibian is found mostly in grassy ponds and wetlands. Little Grass Frogs can jump twenty times their body length. It's identified by its pointy head and dark strip that runs through its eye and down its side.

Discussion

What is your favorite loot to hunt? Who in the Bible gave names to all the animals? What is your favorite animal? Why? How do you show kindness to your pets? Talk about the desire in your heart to be a Mommy or Daddy when you grow up.

From the Bible

"Then God said, 'Let us make man in our image, in our likeness, and let them rule over the fish of the sea and the birds of the air, over the livestock, over all the earth, and over all the creatures that move along the ground.'" Genesis 1:26

"In his hand is the life of every creature and the breath of all mankind." Job 12:10

"A kindhearted woman gains respect." Proverbs 11:16a

"Sons are a heritage from the LORD, children a reward from him." Psalm 127:3

Children, obey your parents in everything, for this pleases the Lord." Colossians 3:20

Song

"All Creatures Of Our God And King" and "Rise And Shine/Arky Arky"

Application

Parents, choose a pet name (nick name) for your child like Dippy Dell in the story (e.g., Love Bug, Honey Bunny, Fast Jack). Draw a picture of a dell. Play Leep Frog. Spend an afternoon at the pet store. Take pictures of all the animals that you see. Research and find out more about one animal. Discover how this animal fits into God's Animal Kingdom.

Idiom

Spic-and-span means spotlessly clean and tidy.

Prayer

Thank the Lord for each member of your family, including your pets.

Chapter 5

Old Gray Mare

"'I tell you,' he replied, 'if they keep
quiet, the stones will cry out.'"

LUKE 19:40

The screech was like the sound of nails running down a blackboard. We heard it coming before we saw it. Sitting on the front porch each evening around five o'clock, I waited for the Old Gray Mare to make its sharp turn around the corner. Once I saw it coming up the black asphalt road, I dashed to the curbside, waiting for the grand, old vehicle to come to a halt. But the grandest thing of all was watching my Daddy step out of the car.

"Daddy, Daddy. Are we going fishing tonight?" These were often the first words from my mouth. Grabbing a big hug, I proceeded to poke and prod, checking to see if just maybe he would have a brown bag containing a styrofoam cup of fat, juicy worms stuffed in his coat pocket.

"Maybe we can go fishing next week," he said, patting me gently as he headed into the house. I longed to hear the words, "We're going fishing today, Lynn Marie."

I followed him like a shadow. "Okay, Daddy, but don't forget." I reminded him as often as I could, like the ticking of a clock. This desire grew each day as I waited faithfully for his return home from work.

It was difficult for my Father to take me fishing because of the old car we had. *"The Old Gray Mare,"* as my Father called the Plymouth, had one seat—a driver's seat. It had been an abandoned car that no one wanted and a gift to our family from a friend. My Father often told us how thankful he was to have a car to drive to work.

I routinely continued to ask my Father to take me fishing. My heart's desire was to be with him even if I was not allowed to talk—when you fish, you have to be quiet or you will scare the fish away. Since I was only five years old, I did not understand why we could not ride in a car without seats. *Who needs a seat?* I thought. It did not seem important to me that the floor boards were so hot that you could not sit on them, as Daddy said.

"Lynn Marie, I'll take you fishing next weekend," Daddy said one day after work.

"Yippie, I can't wait. Don't forget, Daddy!" I recalled those words every day waiting for that great day to arrive. I had my heart and mind fixed on his promise and held tight to the idea that I would soon pitch a pole with my Father. I had forgotten about the need for seats in the Old Gray Mare. I focused on my dream of spending time with my Daddy and trusted that he would take care of all the details.

On Friday evening at five o'clock, my Father was not home yet. My ears were trained for the sound of the squeaky brakes, but tonight he was late. I waited, wondering where he was. *Did he stop to buy some fishing worms?* I asked myself.

A short time later, I could hear the familiar screech in the distance. I bolted from the porch to meet him at the curbside. At a snail-slow pace, the mammoth gray Plymouth came to a complete stop. Out stepped my Daddy with a gentle grin on his face.

"Lynn Marie, why don't you wait for me up at the house?" he directed me. His voice was calm, and I sensed a happy hint of surprise in his tone.

Waiting right inside the front door for his grand entrance, I peered out the window, trying to see what he was doing. It felt like he was out there for an eternity. He was leaning over in the rear of the car with his back to me, blocking the view of his hands.

What could he be doing in the back of the car? I thought. Daddy seemed to be picking up something as if arranging a puzzle on the floor. Finally, up the walkway to the porch he came, and I recoiled from the entrance as if I had been patiently waiting for him. My seemingly long wait looked like it was about to end.

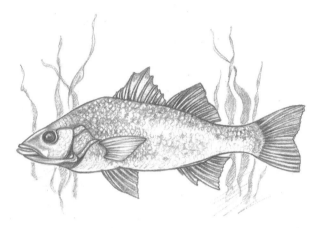

"Come with me, Lynn Marie," he said. Holding my hand, he led me to the car. He opened the door, and there on the floor in the back of the car sat four large cement bricks neatly arranged. Propped against the door beside the bricks, two cane poles stuck their tips out the window, already dressed with bobbers and hooks. On the floor sat a brown paper bag with the fat, juicy worms I had been longing for. For once I was speechless.

"Have a seat," Daddy said, directing me to the bricks, perfectly arranged, almost like real car seats. They were high enough to see out the windows and strong enough to hold a person. What a surprise—seats for the car!

"Are you ready to go fishing now, Little Lady?" Daddy asked with a big grin.

"Yes, Daddy, let's go!" I squealed, feeling like a little princess sitting on her throne. The Old Gray Mare carried us off to my Daddy's favorite fishing hole. It was early evening when we arrived, and dusk was a perfect time to cast a rod. We stayed until dark, catching a bucket full of small perch, enough for a big meal. This was one of many memorable fishing ventures we had together.

Every time I share this story of when I was a little girl I am reminded of the love, care, and dedication that our Heavenly Father has for us. If my earthly Father would go to such efforts to find bricks to make a seat for me, how much more does my heavenly Father want to love me and want to bestow blessings on me? I am affirmed of my heavenly Father's love demonstrated through the love of my earthly Father.

Fishing Tip: Perch fishing is fun and requires the simplest of fishing gear—hook, line, and worm. This tasty catch is abundant in Florida lakes. Perch range from eight to twelve inches in length, or about the size of your hand.

Discussion

How has your Heavenly Father cared for you? What do you admire most about your Father or Grandfather? Do you know of someone who does not have an earthly Father? How could you reach out and show your Heavenly Father's love to them today?

From the Bible

"The living, the living—they praise you, as I am doing today; fathers tell their children about your faithfulness." Isaiah 38:19

"If you, then, though you are evil, know how to give good gifts to your children, how much more will your Father in heaven give good gifts to those who ask him!" Matthew 7:11

"Fathers, do not exasperate your children; instead, bring them up in the training and instruction of the Lord." Ephesians 6:4

Song

"Father We Adore You (Lay Our Lives Before You)" and "How Great Thou Art"

Activity

Collect some rocks or stones to paint, decorate, or make a paper weight. Small children love this! Wrap your work of art, and give it to someone you love. Introduce the old American folk song "The Old Gray Mare." Research its origin.

Application

Plan an activity to do with the special man in your life—your Father, Grandfather, or other loved one. Tell of a favorite pastime you remember with your Father or Grandfather. Remind him that you love him. Surprise your Father by organizing and polishing his shoes.

Idiom

Old Gray Mare refers to something beyond its prime.

Prayer

Thank the Lord for godly men in your life, and praise God for being your Heavenly Father.

Chapter 6

Pierre

*"And whoever welcomes a little child like
this in my name welcomes me."*

Matthew 18:5

We could hear the sound of gravel crunching beneath the tires as we drove down the driveway. Before crossing the small creek, Jeremy had to jump out of the car and roll away a fallen log that was blocking the bridge that led to the main road.

We gradually made our way down the winding road, moving at a snail's pace, hoping to see any interesting wildlife that might be in our path. The crisp fall morning was nippy. We huddled together in the car, waiting for it to warm up.

"Heads up," Jeremy warned. He instructed us to keep our eyes open for a rare and special friend who lived in the forest. "I hope you get to see this little guy," he said excitedly. "I know you'll love him."

Jeremy had spotted this little critter throughout the year, and he was sure he still lived nearby. We had heard about this forest friend for the first time several years back, while visiting Jeremy and his family. Now we eagerly watched for its white hair, white mustache, and white furry tail.

"I want to see him, too," said Kalea, straining to look out the window. We looked all around us, back and forth, hoping to spot the rare wonder.

Out of the corner of my eye, I saw a white flash flutter from log to log, as if it were running home for a hearty meal after hearing the dinner bell.

"What was that?" I cried.

"It's Pierre!" said Jeremy in a tone of voice to let us know that we had better look quickly.

"Where?" asked Kalea, who had known the little rascal her whole four-year-old life.

"Over there, Kalea," Jeremy said, directing our eyes to the rare and dazzling sight. Our wildlife exploration adventure was successful.

Pierre was a white squirrel who had lived on Jeremy's property for several years. Every morning, Jeremy put food in the backyard hoping to get a glimpse of Pierre. "He's spoiled, but we don't mind. He's just like part of the family. *I took a shine to him* the moment I saw him," he explained.

Resting on an old fallen log, a flat tin pan filled with corn and seeds now waited for Pierre and·the other squirrels. Pierre would often make his way through the forest to that small metal dish of food, fill up for the day, and then hop his way back to the woods.

"He doesn't usually play and feed with the other squirrels," Jeremy told us. "I think he's shy."

"Why is he shy, Daddy?" Kalea asked with concern. Jeremy loved her inquisitive questions.

"That's just the way God made him, Sweetie."

"I'm so happy I got to see Pierre," said Kalea, sitting back in her seat satisfied. I thought how odd it was that this beautiful white squirrel lived separate from all the other squirrels.

At a quick glance, one would have to look pretty closely to even know that Pierre was a squirrel. He looked just like a ray of light running through the forest. *Do squirrels gather together to eat, play, and run around through the forest?* I wondered. Why is he not running about with the other squirrels?

There were some similar facts about Pierre and people, facts that really opened up my eyes and made me sit back and think. What was different about the little white squirrel from the other squirrels? He was just a different color. Maybe the other squirrels did not mingle with Pierre because he looked different from them.

I thought about how we treat other people that look different from us. Pierre looked different on the outside, being white as snow, but he was a squirrel just the same.

The Bible says that God loves us no matter how we look on the outside. He made us all just the way we are. Pierre was a beautiful white squirrel and a joy to those who saw him. His difference was what made him so beautiful. We were blessed to catch a glimpse of him that day.

This encounter with Pierre brought back memories from when I was a young girl attending Sunday School at the local church. Every week, the church bus would come to my neighborhood and pick up my brothers, sister, and me for church. One Sunday, sitting in the back of the bus was a young girl. She wore her hair in pigtails, just like me. She was very quiet and seemed a little shy. No one talked to that little girl. When the bus stopped to drop us off at the church, we all piled out and ran into the classroom, but the little girl remained in the back of the bus.

The next week as I ran up the walkway to the church, I glanced back and saw the bus driver helping the same girl out of the bus. When I looked closely, I could see she was in a wheelchair. She could not walk by herself.

To my surprise, the bus driver pushed the little girl into the church and sat her right next to me in Sunday School. I was nervous and a little uncomfortable. Then I remembered how shy I felt my first day at Sunday School, so I offered to share my crayons with her. We colored a picture together, and I found out Rose was a really nice girl, even though she was different from me.

After that day, Rose and I became friends. We started sitting together on the bus each Sunday morning on the way to church. She was just like me—she wanted to have a friend, too. That night I prayed, "Thank you Lord, for sending me my new friend Rose. Help me to show God's love to her."

White squirrels need to be especially alert against predators because of their eye-catching fur color. Squirrels have a strong sense of smell that aids them in locating buried nuts and seeds. Chewing on hard surfaces, such as wood on houses, prevents over-growth of their continually growing sharp teeth. A squirrel's nest is called a drey.

Discussion

In what ways are you blessed because you are different from others? How would you show kindness to someone who is different than you? What are some ways God shows His kindness to you? How can you use your unique differences to "shine" for Jesus?

From the Bible

"I praise you because I am fearfully and wonderfully made; your works are wonderful, I know that full well." Psalm 139:14

"Let love and faithfulness never leave you; bind them around your neck, write them on the tablet of your heart." Proverbs 3:3

"A new command I give you: Love on another. As I have loved you, so you must love one another." John 13:34

Song

"Jesus Loves The Little Children" and "Oh, How He Loves You And Me"

Application

Volunteer to spend time with someone who has a special need. Pray for a caregiver in your family or church and send them a note of encouragement. Offer a helping hand to a younger child who needs encouragement at playtime. Learn to fingerspell (sign language) your favorite song or a common greeting. Craft a poster that reads, KINDNESS MATTERS. Display it as a reminder to treat others with kindness.

Idiom

Take a shine to means to develop a quick fondness.

Prayer

Ask God to help you reflect His love, mercy, and compassion to everyone.

Chapter 7

Boy, Ben, and Bass

*"Then he took the seven loaves and the fish, and when
he had given thanks, he broke them and gave them
to the disciples, and they in turn to the people."*

MATTHEW 15:36

"Boy, Boy, where's the Boy?" We were sitting in our living room when we heard someone calling. It sounded like the noise was coming from our front porch. Looking out the window, we saw a lady standing on the other side of the fence. I knew there was an older couple that lived next door, but we had never met them. They seemed reclusive, wanting to be left alone. Alex was just two years old at the time. This was the first opportunity to introduce ourselves to the seemingly shy neighbors who appeared on the scene.

"Hello there, Boy," the little lady called. We approached the fence to greet our neighbor. The little lady reached over the fence to rub Alex on the head. Not far behind her followed a man.

"What's your name, Boy?" Alex squirmed in my arms as the lady reached over the fence.

"Alex," he quickly answered, turning his face sheepishly away from them. *She must have seen us playing in the yard or walking in the neighborhood,* I thought.

"Boy, you're such a Big Boy!" she said peering side to side to get a peek at his little face.

The neighbor's yard was overgrown with bushes covering the windows, and a web of vines crawled up the side of the house like a jungle. For some time I thought no one lived there. I was surprised that they came to the fence. The only activity I ever saw was the man pulling a small fishing boat in and out of the driveway.

"Hi, my name is Ben, and this is Mary Lou," the man said as he gently put his arm around his wife.

"Hello, I'm Lynn Marie, and we're both pleased to meet you." We stood at the fence for a few minutes and talked. It was small talk between neighbors who had just met, but we were happy to get acquainted.

After meeting Ben and Mary Lou, we noticed them outside in the front of their house more regularly. When we walked past their house, they would often say hello. Mary Lou always referred to Alex as "The Boy," a nickname she gave him. They always seemed happy to see us.

One day, as we passed our neighbors in the yard, I noticed they looked like they needed some home cooking and tender loving care. I believe God gave me the idea to take Mary Lou and Ben a cherry cobbler. They received the warm dish jubilantly and gratefully. That day marked the beginning of our friendship.

Not long after that, our neighbor Ben came walking up to our carport with a metal bucket in each hand. "Howdy there, do you like fish?" he asked with a big smile.

"Yes, we sure do," I answered. *Maybe I should see what's in the buckets before I answer so quickly,* I thought, but the words were already out of my mouth. The buckets were full of flip-floppin' fish that were spilling water in every direction.

"What kind of fish are they?" I asked.

"Bass," Ben answered, looking proud of his big catch.

"What are you going to do with all these fish?" I questioned, not imagining his answer would have anything to do with us.

"Some of these fish are for you and Alex. Fish will be good for the Boy."

I swallowed with a big gulp and asked, "Are those fish for us?"

"Yes, Ma'am," Ben said smiling back. "Come over here and pick out some pretty ones. Then we can clean 'em."

Oh no! I thought. *Clean fish?* "But Ben, I don't know how to clean fish. How would I hold down one of those slippery, smelly, squirmy creatures, much less clean one?"

"Come on Lynn, you can do it," said Ben, and he was prepared to show me how. He pulled our picnic table over to the edge of the carport and reached into his canvas satchel, pulling out a long, slender leather case. It contained an instrument for filleting fish.

"I'll be right back. I'm going home to get some old newspapers. Don't go away," he insisted.

What will I do with two buckets of fish? I thought. Now I was the *fish out of water*! In no time, Ben was back with a stack of newspapers just like he said. By now, Alex was up to his elbows with the smelly catch, wanting to hold every one of them. Ben spread newspaper across the picnic table. He proceeded to show me how to gut and fillet the freshwater bass, instructing me each step of the way.

"Don't be shy now, come over here and watch. It's not hard," Ben directed.

"Okay, Ben, I'll give it my *best shot!*"

The smelly, wet drippings ran off the table and dribbled down the carport to the grass. I had not seen anything like this since I was a little girl when my Father used to clean his fish. But that was so long ago, and he cleaned the fish back then, not me.

Soon, Mary Lou arrived offering a box of plastic baggies to store the fresh fillets. Mary Lou and Ben stayed the afternoon to show me how to cook the fish. They had a secret recipe, so I felt special that they shared it with me. The fish was well worth the work.

We began to recognize the sound of Ben's truck coming down the road with the small boat he towed. Alex would run to the fence, waiting to see if Ben took any buckets out of the boat.

"Fish, fish, the fish are here," Alex called out, pointing over the fence. Sometimes Ben came back with empty buckets, but that was a rare occasion.

"Come here, Boy," Ben summoned. "Come and look at these pretty fish."

We always looked forward to the fish that Ben would bring us. The fishy meals tasted good in our mouths and filled our bellies. With God's help, I overcame my fear and learned to clean fish. There was not a catch that I could not fillet. Ben taught me well. We never lacked for fresh fish over the next two summers. Our freezer was always full of little baggies of mouth-watering fillets. Mary Lou and Ben made sure we always had part of the fresh catch of the day.

We are grateful to the Lord that He brought our families together this way. My heart was touched by the generosity of this sweet couple. We later called him Uncle Ben as he requested. Uncle Ben and Mary Lou were like family, and we loved them very much. We shared many fish dinners together.

This was over twenty years ago, and although Uncle Ben and Mary Lou have passed away, we have remained friends with the rest of their family.

Fishing tip: Bass feed in shallow water very early and very late in the day. Bass can get as large as twenty pounds. Cast your rod where bass love to hide—near rock piles, weeds, and logs that extend into the water.

Discussion

How did God demonstrate His provision throughout this story? Learning to clean fish can be intimidating. Is there a daunting challenge facing you today? How can courage help you tackle a new undertaking? Do you have a neighbor you have not met yet? What do you have that you could share with that neighbor?

Scripture

"Let them give thanks to the LORD for his unfailing love and his wonderful deeds for men, for he satisfies the thirsty and fills the hungry with good things." Psalm 107:8–9

"The entire law is summed up in a single command: 'Love your neighbor as yourself.'" Galatians 5:14

"For God did not give us a spirit of timidity, but a spirit of power, of love and of self-discipline." 2 Timothy 1:7

Song

"Fishers Of Men" and "Praise To The Lord, The Almighty"

Application

Host a fish fry. Learn about basic food preparation techniques, such as safety, sanitation, and spoilage. Bake a fresh cobbler for your neighbor. Assemble a small fish aquarium or fish bowl and study tropical fish. Research the different species of fish that are native to your area. Go fishing and have a picnic at your favorite pond.

Idiom

Fish out of water means someone feels out of place.
Best shot means do the best you can.

Prayer

Thank the Lord for the bountiful provisions of food, clothing, and shelter that He provides each day.

Chapter 8

Paper Trail

*"Now it is required that those who have
been given a trust must prove faithful."*

1 CORINTHIANS 4:2

The church we attended needed volunteers to deliver meals to the shut-ins of the community. Many elderly only enjoyed a hot meal when it was brought to them. I had been praying for an opportunity for our family to serve at our local church.

"Could you and Alex help out at the church today? We're short-handed," a friend called to ask.

"Sure, we'd love to help. We'll see you at the church," I said. I was thrilled to get the call.

We would first have to go by the church to pick up the meals. The meals were prepared that morning in the church kitchen and put into plastic carriers to keep them warm. When we arrived, there was a lady in the lobby writing out name tags.

"Hello there. How old are you, Little Fella?" asked the kind lady with a pen in her hand.

"I am five years old," Alex softly answered.

She patted a sticky white name tag onto his chest as I picked up the map that listed our assigned territory for that day. "I believe the Lord has a very special plan for today," I told Alex as we got back into the car and said a prayer. "Lord, please lead us to someone who needs help."

I looked on the map to see where our first stop would be. Our route was off a busy road in an old apartment complex. The neighborhood was not too far from the church, but it was a part of town unfamiliar to me. We walked from door to door delivering the hot meals.

"Oh, how wonderful," said one elderly man, opening the door and patting Alex on the head, "not just for the food, but how wonderful it is to meet you. Come inside and see my cat, Precious." He was happy to tell us about his pet cat. Alex also enjoyed playing with the cat before we moved to the next name on the list.

Several of the people we visited that day told us about their deep faith in God. It was an encouragement to hear people of life-long faith talk about the God that we had read about in the Bible. "That man looked like Moses in the Bible," Alex told me, thinking of the older gentleman with a beard we had just visited.

What a blessing to witness that the same God of the Bible who cared for the sick and the hungry was providing for the needs of these people today. We came to the last name on our list and knocked on the door. We knocked and knocked, but no one answered.

"Maybe no one's home," Alex said. I put my face next to the door and gently called, "Mrs. Prescott." No one answered.

"Is someone coming, Mommy?" Alex curiously asked. The door slowly creeped open. It sounded like it was stuck. Nothing could have prepared us for what we were about to see on the other side of the door.

"Oh, someone's home!" peeped Alex.

Through the halfway-opened door, we saw an elderly lady in a wheelchair. She was trying her best to open the door all the way, but it kept knocking on the bottom of her chair. With our help, she was finally able to swing open the door.

"Oh, my," she exclaimed, surprised to see strangers standing there. Her shoulders were slumped over, and she could hardly lift her head to look at us. Her hair was snarled and uncombed. She looked very unhealthy and sad.

"I'm so glad to see somebody today," she said as she started to weep. Alex stood there and listened quietly. "Thank you, young man," she replied, as she reached out to shake his hand.

"You're welcome, Ma'am. Nice to meet you, too," Alex replied.

"I've been alone here ill for sometime praying that someone would come and help me," she said softly.

"You are the answer to our prayer," I told her. "God led us to you."

This must be the providence of God, I thought. I remembered that we prayed for the Lord to lead us that day. This lady was alone and needed help. We stayed and visited with her for a while and gave her a hot meal when we left.

I believed in my heart that God had answered that prayer. The end of our visit came quickly. It was a *bittersweet* farewell, because we did not want to leave our new friend; we had to trust that God would send someone to help her.

"Who will take care of her, Mommy?" Alex asked on our way back to the car. "God will take care of her, Sweetheart. Let's pray. Dear God, please show us how to help this poor lady. In Jesus' name, Amen."

After finishing our meal deliveries, we went to my office where I worked part time as a clerk for an attorney. I was in the back room doing my usual organizing and filing of the large amounts of documents that daily came into the office. I moved through pile after pile. As I made my way through the trail of papers, I descended upon a particular stack that caught my eye (though I still do not know why it did).

As I started to file the stack, I looked down and realized that the paper I was holding had the name Mrs. Prescott, the very same name as the lady we had met that morning. After close examination, I discovered that the address was also the same as the apartment where we had been.

I rushed down the hall to the attorney's office with the paper in hand. Together we searched out the case and found it had been set aside for some unknown reason. He thanked me for bringing this timely issue to his attention. I ran back to tell Alex the news.

"Look, Alex, this letter is about Mrs. Prescott, the lady we visited today. With this information we can get her all the help she needs."

"Yippee!" Alex shouted. We danced around the filing room celebrating.

We later discovered that Mrs. Prescott had been waiting for this very important paper so that she could get medical attention. The Lord led us directly to Mrs. Prescott's house and then He led my hands directly to that stack of papers. Within hours, there was a nurse at her home to take care of her, and she recovered completely.

God hears the prayers of his children. We are grateful for the honor and privilege of serving Mrs. Prescott that day. This experience became a memorial in our hearts of answered prayer.

"For I was hungry and you gave me something to eat, I was thirsty and you gave me something to drink, I was a stranger and you invited me in, I needed clothes and you clothed me, I was sick and you looked after me." Matthew 25:35–38

Discussion

Can you name one important responsibility that God has entrusted to you? How can prayer encourage you to meet your daily responsibilities? Can you retrace the trail of prayers in this story? Can you give an example of how Jesus put the needs of others before His own? What are you willing to forgo in order to fulfill the needs of others?

From the Bible

"Your love, O LORD, reaches to the heavens, your faithfulness to the skies." Psalm 36:5

"O Lord, hear my prayer, listen to my cry for mercy; in your faithfulness and righteousness come to my relief." Psalm 143:1

"For even the Son of Man did not come to be served, but to serve, and to give his life as a ransom for many." Mark 10:45

Song

"Standing In The Need Of Prayer" and "There Is A Balm In Gilead"

Application

Role-play the story of the Good Samaritan in Luke 10:33–35. Maybe you know someone who needs a hot meal or just a friendly visit. Make a name tag and write on it, "I'm blessed." Wear it when you serve others, and when people ask you about it, tell them why you are so blessed. Play "Paper Trail." Write little notes of appreciation or affection, and place them under pillows, on mirrors, and other obscure places to be discovered. Your family will be encouraged.

Idiom

Bittersweet means regret happens alongside benefit.

Prayer

Pray for an opportunity for your family to serve in any place or in any way that God leads you.

Chapter 9

Treasure Walk

"For where your treasure is, there your heart will be also."

MATTHEW 6:21

When I was a young girl, I used to walk home from school on one of the most beautiful, scenic roads in the world. The entire street looked like a movie set because of its lush landscape and beautiful old homes. I recall, as if it were yesterday, how carefree I felt walking up and down the old brick road of that neighborhood. Looking upward with wonder and peering through the thick oak trees that canopied the charming road, I imagined what it would be like to live in such a magnificent corner of the world.

I never told anyone about my girlish desire, but God knew. I forgot about the wishful dream until twenty years later when I would indeed live right in that same neighborhood, paved by the same red brick that I walked on as a child. This would be the place I would raise my son for the first sixteen years of his life. This would be the home of some of our happiest memories.

"Mommy, will you please read to me about the little raccoon?" Holding the book under his arm, Alex ran across the room, landing in my lap ready to settle down for his favorite story. He was just five years old, and I read this story to him almost every day.

The story was about a little raccoon who lived outside under the trees. While he was playing there, acorns fell, hitting him on the head. "Tap, tap," they fell right on his furry little head.

"Mommy, will you please tap me on the head, too, like the little raccoon?" He asked me to tap him on his head every time I read this story as if an acorn were falling on his head just like in the book.

"Will you read it one more time?" he would ask, and I read it to him again and again. He giggled with each little tap on his head; he thought this was so funny.

"Let's go for a walk," I said one morning after reading the raccoon story.

"Maybe we'll see a raccoon today," Alex said with anticipation. The road in front of our house was lined with huge oak trees that we called Papa Oaks because they were so large. While strolling down the road that day, Alex suddenly stopped in his tracks and knelt down, having discovered some acorns on the ground. He was so excited.

"Look, Mommy, acorns—just like in the raccoon story." His eyes were as brown and round as the acorns he was holding.

"It's so wonderful to walk outside and then, just moments later, have in your hands the very thing you were just reading about," I said to him.

"I'm so glad I have acorn pouches," Alex said pointing to the big pockets of his old, favorite jeans. The holes in the knees did not keep him from kneeling down and gathering the acorns he saw on the ground that day. He left *no stone unturned* in search of the little nuts.

"Crunch" went the acorns as I tip-toed about as cautiously as I could. Alex called out, "Careful, Mommy, please don't step on the treasure." We had discovered something of great value and meaning to him.

"Okay, Little One. I'll be careful," reassuring him that his loot would be safe. Like a little raccoon with his cheeks full of acorns, Alex filled his pockets full of the little hard nuts.

The branches of the Papa Oaks were weighed down with the brown, nutty delights. Every few steps we would bend down, searching for the best acorns, the well-rounded ones, with the kernel and shell still intact. There were acorns everywhere we looked, but the best ones were the hardest to find.

We headed back to the house, and Alex ran straight to the kitchen table. He slipped his small hands into his stuffed pockets to retrieve the valuable gems. He stood by the table and examined the acorns one by one, placing them carefully on the table, making sure that they did not roll onto the floor.

"Mommy, these acorns are just like finding treasure!" he cheered with fascination.

"Yes, Son, the acorns are like treasure; they are treasure just like you! God made acorns so that we could have lots of beautiful trees like the big Papa Oak trees."

Unhurried, he continued picking up each acorn one at a time, discovering that no two were alike.

"Just like the acorns, Alex, you are one of a kind, there is no one else like you," I told him. "You are treasured by God and by me. Like the little acorns that grow into magnificent oak trees, you are growing up into a unique and special person."

"I want to be big and strong like the big Papa Oaks," he said with all his child-like might.

"We'll pray that you'll grow up to be everything that God wants you to be," I assured him with a smile. Alex beamed as he pushed his collected treasure into a little pile on the table. An ordinary walk ended with an extraordinary glimpse of our hope and future. As a mother, that glimpse was worth more than a pot of gold.

Our "treasure walks" were our choice pastimes. The seeds of encouragement planted in our hearts during our walks together have grown into many cherished memories.

I saved those acorns from that day in a little silver cup that still sits on my dresser. As Alex gathered treasure in his pockets, I gathered treasure in my heart from the time we spent together. To capture our little one's hearts and discover priceless treasure with them, we do not have to travel far, and the only cost is our time and affection.

Another name for acorn is oak nut. Acorns are one of the most important wildlife foods in areas where there are oak trees. Raccoons, squirrels, deer, and birds depend on acorns as a source of food. Acorns can be stored for over twenty-five years. Dotori-muk is the name of a Korean jelly made of acorns.

Discussion

What is one of your greatest treasures? How do you like to spend treasured time with your family? How have you witnessed God display His splendor? How can we nurture the treasure of God's Word in our hearts? How has God shown you that you are treasured by Him?

From the Bible

"Delight yourself in the LORD and he will give you the desires of your heart." Psalm 37:4

"They will be called oaks of righteousness, a planting of the LORD for the display of his splendor." Isaiah 61:3b

"The kingdom of heaven is like treasure hidden in a field. When a man found it, he hid it again, and then in his joy went and sold all he had and bought that field." Matthew 13:44

Song

"You Shall Go Out With Joy (The Trees Of The Fields)" and "He's Got The Whole World In His Hands"

Application

Go for a "treasure walk" with your children, and you will be surprised at all the little gems you discover. Record what you find. Make a treasure map and draw out your favorite paths. Plan a "treasure hunt" (inside or outside) hiding little tokens of joy for your loved ones to uncover. Spending time like this can be a fun way to convey to your children their value to you and to God. Collect acorns and make a tambourine or shaker.

Idiom

No stone unturned means to exhaust all efforts in search of something.

Prayer

Ask the Lord to reveal to you the treasure you already possess. Then thank Him for creating that treasure.

Chapter 10

Letting Go

"Each man should give what he has decided in his heart to give, not reluctantly or under compulsion, for God loves a cheerful giver."

2 CORINTHIANS 9:7

Alex came running from the backyard. "I tore my pants on the glider again," he cried. He was very attached to his swing set and played on it almost every day; but he had outgrown it for some time now, and I decided it was time to give it away.

"Come inside, Little Guy, and let me take a look at that hole," I said, comforting him.

"Okay, Mommy. Don't forget, those are my favorite jeans." Alex loved his old blue jeans, and he wore them every chance he could. I went to his bedroom and pulled from his dresser a pair of crisp, white pants and exchanged them for the torn jeans. Alex settled for the substitute pants for the time being but sat right beside me until I finished mending the torn favorites.

The interruption of the morning incident soon passed, and all was well. I hung Alex's favorite pants neatly on a hook in his closet. That evening, as I was tucking him in, he thanked me for mending his jeans. This was an opportunity for me to break the news to him. He had outgrown the swing set, and we needed to find it a new home.

"Son, why do you think you tore your pants on the swing set again?"

"Because they caught on the seat?" he answered.

"Alex, you've outgrown the swing set, and your clothes are catching on it because you're getting so big." As I sat by his bed I explained, "When we grow up, sometimes we have to let go of things. One day, Alex, very soon, you will not be able to fit into those jeans either no matter how many times I sew them up."

The next day, I stood at the kitchen window and watched Alex play in the back yard. I remembered when my father had bought that swing set for Alex's second birthday. It had blessed us with many hours of fun. The memories were extra special because "Papa" had often been outside with us, too. Alex was quite tall for a six-year-old, and now the gray metal contraption wobbled and threatened to tip when he squeezed his body into it.

When I talked about the possibility of giving the swing set to someone, Alex would plead, "Can I keep it just one more day, please?" It seemed impossible to say no.

"Okay, just one more day, and then we have to give it to another child." Not being able to resist his earnest appeals, I repeatedly consented.

"Alex, why don't you want to give the swing set away? I don't want you to get hurt on it." He started to cry.

"Mommy, Papa gave that swing set to me, and I want to keep it forever."

I patiently listened and then said, "Alex, letting go is sometimes hard, especially when we are growing up. Papa would understand. He would be so proud of how big you are. Papa would be pleased that you shared this swing set with someone else. I understand how you feel, Son."

"It's the most special swing set in the whole world," Alex cried. We shared a precious moment remembering our sweet Papa, who was no longer with us. I wiped his tears away.

"Alex, let's pray right now that we can find someone who would really like to have a swing set, someone who's not able to buy one." He perked right up in an instant.

"That's a great idea, Mommy." He tightly held my hand and prayed. "Lord Jesus, help us to find a special boy or girl who needs a swing set. Please send them our way. Thank you, Jesus, Amen."

I was not quite sure if he would change his mind the next morning. When I went into his room, I found him putting on his favorite old jeans. "Good morning, Sunshine! Are you ready to start the day?"

"Mommy, are we still going to give the swing set away?" he immediately asked.

"Alex, remember, we prayed that we could find someone who needs a swing set?"

"Yes, Mommy, I remember." I assured him once more that we would be able to bless someone else. He seemed to accept the idea that we would be finding a new home for the play set.

We scrubbed the swing set to a sparkle, and made sure every nut and bolt were tight. We then called on George, our neighbor, to come over and help us carry the swing set to the front yard. We put a sign on it that read, "Free." No sooner was the sign on display than I heard a car pull up to the curb. A woman and a small boy got out of the car. "Are you giving the swing set away?" she asked as if she could hardly believe it.

"Yes, it's free if you'd like it," I told her.

Holding her little boy's hand, she smiled and said, "We'd love to have it. We have wanted one for some time." Her son was three years old, and the swing set fit him perfectly. The mother and her little boy came back that afternoon with a truck and picked up their new swing set. It was a *match made in heaven*. Everyone was pleased.

We celebrated that evening knowing that our beloved swing set had found a new home. Seeing this little boy's face when he got his new swing set made the "letting go" more like "giving to."

"Mommy, can you believe that God sent that little boy here, just like we prayed?"

"Yes, Alex, I believe it. God hears all of our prayers. I am so happy that someone else can have fun with the swing set and make happy memories."

"I think Papa would be happy, too." added Alex.

"Let's also think about this, Alex. Just like you 'let go' of your special swing set, God 'let go' of His special Son," I explained. "God sent Jesus to die for us on the cross so that we could live with Him forever."

That night at bedtime, we prayed, "Thank you, God, for sending your only Son to die for us. Thank you for 'letting go' of Jesus, to save us. Amen."

Not long after we gave the swing set away, Alex outgrew his favorite jeans. I had patched all the patches I could patch. We finally had to throw them away. But soon afterward, the Lord was gracious to Alex blessing him with a new pair of jeans for which he was very grateful.

"Our Father which art in heaven, Hallowed be thy name. Thy kingdom come, Thy will be done in earth, as it is in heaven. Give us this day our daily bread. And forgive us our debts, as we forgive our debtors. And lead us not into temptation, but deliver us from evil: For thine is the kingdom, and the power, and the glory, for ever. Amen." Matthew 6:9–13 KJV

Discussion

Why did God "let go" of Jesus to come to earth? What is one way we can show our gratitude to God for sending Jesus to die for us? Can you name one sacrifice your parents have made for you, which you are grateful for? Have you ever "let go" of something to bless someone else?

From the Bible

"He guides the humble in what is right and teaches them his way." Psalm 25:9

"For where two or three come together in my name, there am I with them." Matthew 18:20

"For God so loved the world that he gave his one and only Son, that whoever believes in him shall not perish but have eternal life." John 3:16

"It is more blessed to give than to receive." Acts 20:35b

Song

"The Lord's Prayer" and "Near To The Heart Of God"

Application

Fill a basket with items from your room or closet that you no longer use. Let each child choose two items of their own that they want to give, or let go. If they have outgrown larger toys such as bikes, swings, or wagons, then first paint or clean them. This is a fun family project that will reap great benefits for all. Pray and ask the Lord to lead you to a family to bless with the refurbished items. You may also choose to donate them anonymously.

Idiom

Match made in heaven means two things go together perfectly

Prayer

Thank God for giving His only special Son Jesus to die for us.

Chapter 11

One Little Indian Boy

"God sets the lonely in families..."

PSALM 68:6

Fall had always been our favorite time of year. As soon as the calendar page turned over to September, I made sure there was a big pumpkin and a pot of bright yellow mums on the front porch.

"Mom, are we going to make a scarecrow again this year?" asked Alex.

"We sure are, Alex. How about a farmer scarecrow? " I replied.

"Okay, Mommy, that's a great idea!"

To add to the festive look of fall, we stuffed some old clothes with straw and made our own scarecrow that looked like a farmer. The front porch now welcomed any guests that came our way.

By the time Alex was four years old, both of my parents had passed away. There was a "Grandparent" void in our lives, and as a Mom, I felt helpless to fill that void. I wondered how I would teach Alex to respect and honor the elderly. This was heavy on my heart and in the forefront of my mind.

One Saturday my friend Julie called. "Do you and Alex want to go with me to visit my Mom today?"

"We'd love to," I quickly replied.

Julie knew we loved to visit her Mother, Marie, whom we called "Gramma Marie." She was always working on fun craft projects. Alex also liked to go because he was sure to get a piece of chocolate candy from the tin box that sat on the piano in the parlor.

This particular afternoon, while we were visiting, she pulled out a paper sack and showed us the pattern of an old Indian costume that she had made for Julie when she was a little girl. Alex's eyes got big when he saw the picture of the colorful costume.

"Mommy, do you think you could make me an Indian costume like this?" he asked eagerly. I started thinking about how much fun it would be to make a costume for Alex.

I turned to Marie and asked, "Could you help us make a costume? Do you have the time?"

With a big smile on her face, she replied, "I'd love to help you. Let's start right away."

For several weeks, we went to Gramma Marie's house in the afternoons and helped work on the Indian costume. Threading the colorful, tiny beads for the trim, Alex exclaimed, "This looks like real Indian chief clothes, Mommy!"

He was fascinated by the work of art and wanted to try on the outfit every time we visited. He loved to see, feel, and hear the beads that dangled and jingled down his sides when he jumped up and down. The best part of the project was spending time with Gramma Marie. She was like family to us.

The costume was finally completed. We all sat in Gramma's parlor watching Alex's grand performance of "One Little Indian Boy" while he went prancing, dancing, and chanting around the make-believe campfire in the middle of the room. The celebration finished with a piece of Gramma's famous chocolate candy.

"Gramma Marie, thank you so much," Alex said hugging her tightly.

"I never want to take this off!" he declared.

He put the colorfully decorated costume on in the mornings when he woke up, and some days he even wanted to sleep in it. It was rewarding and fun seeing how much this Indian outfit meant to him as well as having memories of the hours spent with Gramma Marie.

Soon after this, the Lord put on my heart to take my little Indian to visit a nursing home in our neighborhood. When I called the nursing home, they told us we were more than welcome to visit.

"Oh, please come and visit," bid the friendly nurse. "The residents here will *get a kick out of* meeting a real Indian boy."

I explained to Alex that many elderly in nursing homes do not have family or friends visiting them, and they are very lonely. Alex was thrilled to have the chance to wear his costume in a new place.

I painted Alex's face like an Indian chief. On his head, I tied the colorful feather headpiece we had made to go along with the outfit. "Okay, Big Chief, are you ready to go?" I invited with delight.

"HOW! BIG CHIEF IS READY," he said, raising his hand. "Let's race; I'll beat you to the car!"

Our first visit at the nursing home was during lunchtime. We carried a bag filled with games and books to entertain the residents, but all they wanted was to meet the little boy with the colorful costume.

"Here he comes," they called out as Alex walked around the room, shaking hands with each person. He pulled a chair right up to the table in the dining room and sat down.

"I caught my biggest fish ever!" Alex exclaimed, as he proceeded to tell the captive audience about his most recent fishing adventure. All eyes were on the little Indian boy as he told the exaggerated story of the greatest catch of his life. When he was done, they threw up their hands and cheered, rubbed his little head, and shook his little hand. They did not want him to leave.

"I'll be back to see you soon," Alex assured them as we departed. Some days he did not want to leave their side. He was happy just spending time with all his many "Grandparents."

Our visits to the nursing home became more frequent as we came to know the staff and residents. The nurses told us that the people would ask, "When is the little Indian boy coming?" During the holidays, we were able to spend a lot more time visiting our new friends.

We learned to be grateful for the elderly. The rich experience of spending time listening to them, loving them, and comforting them came back to bless us. We still talk about those times and those people today.

God did not overlook the void in our lives and the desire in our hearts for grandparents. He gave us Gramma Marie, who spent endless hours with Alex, showing the love and affection that a little boy yearns for. The people at the nursing home blessed us by sharing their wisdom, their time, and their love with us.

There is not a need that goes unnoticed by our Heavenly Father. He sees all things, knows all things, and desires to give us all good things.

"A father to the fatherless, a defender of widows, is God in his holy dwelling. God sets the lonely in families, he leads forth the prisoners with singing, but the rebellious live in a sun-scorched land." Psalm 68:5–6

Discussion

What is your favorite pastime with your grandparents? Can you recall an instance when the Lord has filled a special need in your life through someone close to you? Do you know of someone with a specific void in their life to whom you can minister? How can you show respect to others? What fall tradition is most memorable or meaningful to you?

From the Bible

"Is not wisdom found among the aged? Does not long life bring understanding?" Job 12:12

"But the needy will not always be forgotten, nor the hope of the afflicted ever perish." Psalm 9:18

"A generous man will prosper; he who refreshes others will himself be refreshed." Proverbs 11:25

"Gray hair is a crown of splendor, it is attained by a righteous life." Proverbs 16:31

Song

"Ten Little Indian Boys" and "Heavenly Sunshine"

Application

Pack a sack of fun activities, and visit a nursing home. Ask the residents to tell you their favorite story. They will love your undivided attention. You may want to dress up in one of your favorite costumes. Take a pot of pretty mums or a box of chocolates to bless someone who is lonely. Make a colorful Indian costume or headdress, and play Cowboys and Indians.

Idiom

Get a kick out of means to get great enjoyment from something.

Prayer

Thank God for those special people in your life who teach you wisdom.

Chapter 12

Decision Revision Provision

"Shouts of joy and victory resound in the tents of the righteous: "The Lord's right hand has done mighty things!"

PSALM 118:15

The first time I heard about the church camping trip was when I read about it in the bulletin. We had never been on a camping trip. The fact that this would be at Disney World made it look more inviting. The most appealing part, however, was that we would be with other families from the church. Our church families did everything together.

"Announcements, please; everybody look in your bulletin with me at the upcoming events." The pastor called to our attention the plans for the church camping trip. Sometimes I would wait to tell Alex about upcoming events until just the right time, but not today. The pastor beat me to it.

"Mom, are we going camping at Disney World?" It would have been nice if I could have said yes right then.

"I'm not sure right now, Alex; it's several weeks away. But we will sure pray about it."

I hoped to find out whether a camping trip would be possible in the coming days. A trip like this with our church family was something Alex and I had always talked about doing.

There was a sign-up sheet at church the following week. It was too soon for me to make the commitment. I wanted to be able to take Alex, but I did not want to get his hopes up.

"Would you and Alex like to go camping?" asked our friend Mr. Hunt.

"We'd love to go, but I'll have to let you know next week." I was seriously considering the idea.

"Okay, let us know. We'll save you a spot just in case." said Mr. Hunt. He was a faithful servant who kept us informed of the church happenings.

There was a lot to consider before I could say yes. The revision of my work schedule and the provision of a tent for us had to be considered; then, finally, the decision to take the leap of faith to make the commitment. I spent the next night dedicating these needs to the Lord.

Alex had a small pup tent that was given to him for his birthday. He set it up in his room for when he played Indians, but tonight he just wanted to sleep in it. I stuck my head inside the tent and watched him sleep. His body alone filled the tiny tent. I imagined how much fun it would be to go on a real camping trip, but I could not see how it would come together.

I knelt beside the tent and said a quiet prayer. *Lord, I so much want to take Alex on this camping trip, but I will need Your help to work out the details. Please make a way for us to go if it's your will. I thank you in advance, in Jesus' name, Amen.* I would now be able to rest since I had entrusted this to the Lord.

The following week was the deadline to reserve a campsite. I requested time off from my weekend job but had not heard back. The church agreed to hold a spot for us even if we were not sure we could go. There was still the issue of finding a tent big enough for us. Most of the families from church were going on the trip, so borrowing a tent was not an option. Buying a tent for two nights was also out of the question.

Time was running out, and I needed to make a decision about the camping trip. I was not able to get off from work, so I would not be able to go on the trip. A family from our church offered for Alex to join them. Breaking the news to him would be difficult.

"Alex, I know you really want to go on the church camping trip."

"Oh yes, Mommy, I am so excited! Are we going?"

"I have good news for you, Son. You get to go camping with the Pent family. They have a big RV and they said they would love for you to go with them." He smiled at first, and then looked at the ground.

"But, Mom, it won't be as fun without you," he said sadly.

"Look at the bright side, Alex. You'll have a wonderful time with Mr. Pent and his boys. You can all go fishing and swimming." I assured him that it was okay for him to go without me.

The group met at four o'clock on Friday afternoon and caravanned to Disney World. I promised Alex that I would join him at the church service on Sunday morning at the campgrounds. It meant a lot to me that he would be spending time with the other church families. "Have a wonderful time. I hope you catch a big fish!" As we hugged and said our good-byes, I was grateful that he got to go camping.

After dropping Alex off at the church, I went home to eat dinner. There was a message waiting for me on my answering machine. It was my boss.

"Lynn, this is Betty. We will be using the offices for meetings all weekend. You won't be able to come in and clean. You'll have to come early next week to clean the offices. I hope you have a nice weekend."

Her words were *music to my ears*. Now I could join Alex at the campsite. He would be so surprised. But where would I sleep? There were no arrangements for me to camp, and it would be late when I arrived.

As I contemplated my dilemma, I went into Alex's room to get a duffle bag from his closet and tripped over the small tent that was set up in the middle of the bedroom. I paused and stared at it. Could I fit in that little tent for a night?

Yes, I could! I thought. I quickly disassembled the tent. With my duffle bag in hand and the tiny tent in arm, I headed out for the campsite. When I arrived it was pitch dark. Only a few light flickers burned nearby. The night patrol directed me to the site where the Pent family was registered.

Their RV was dark, and they were all asleep. Slowly I pulled my car up next to the site, being careful not to slam the car door. I pitched my tent right next to the RV. The only sound was the crunching of the gravel under my feet as I walked around setting up the little tent. It was a cinch to put together, so no one heard me. I was *quiet as a mouse*.

It was very early the following morning when the campers began to stir. The smell of bacon and fresh coffee filled the air. I was awakened by the sound of feet hitting the gravel from the RV next to me.

"Mother!" Alex screamed. I felt the ground tremble as he dashed over to the tent. "When did you get here?" he asked, frantically unzipping the window of the tent. I do not remember ever seeing him so excited or surprised. A small crowd had now gathered to see who was in the tiny tent. I crawled my way out and surprised everyone when they discovered it was me inside.

"I wouldn't have missed this for the world," I announced, looking at our quaint group. Alex hugged me and smiled, "Mom, this is the best surprise in the whole world!"

The gravel was a little tough to sleep on, but besides that, we had a wonderful weekend. The Lord was gracious to bring our circumstances together. I made the decision for the trip, my boss made the revision to my schedule, and the provision of the tent we had all along.

Through this experience, God taught me that noble desires are worth the extra effort. The big events we plan do not always fulfill us as we imagine they would. It is the simplest joys in life that end up meaning the most.

"In a large house there are articles not only of gold and silver, but also of wood and clay; some are for noble purposes and some for ignoble." 2 Timothy 2:20

Discussion

Is there something special you would like to accomplish but think it looks too difficult? Are you placing your desires in God's hands, trusting him for the outcome? What small sacrifices could you make to accomplish your goal? What does "noble" mean? Do you have noble desires for your family and for God?

Scripture

"Offer right sacrifices and trust in the Lord." Psalm 4:5

"For the Lord is good and his love endures forever, his faithfulness continues through all generations." Psalm 100:5

"And we know that all things work together for good to them that love God, to them who are the called according to his purpose." Romans 8:28

"However, as it is written: 'No eye has seen, no ear has heard, no mind has conceived what God has prepared for those who love him.'" 1 Corinthians 2:9

Song

"Kum Ba Ya" and "I'd Rather Have Jesus"

Application

Plan a family camping trip (or backyard overnighter) using only the "bare necessities" that you already possess. You could make S'mores or mountain pies. Invite another family for friend to join you. Honor the Lord by sharing your provisions with your guests. Play a game of "Hot Potato" around a circle. Your noble efforts will make many happy memories.

Idiom

Music to my ears means good news.
Quiet as a mouse means subdued; making very little noise.

Prayer

Thank the Lord for your church family. Bless the Lord with thanksgiving for all the ways He provides for you.

Chapter 13

Hooks, Lines, and Stingers

"Is any one of you in trouble? He should pray."

JAMES 5:13A

Most Saturday mornings, I awoke with feelings of anticipation. The busy weekends typically included a brand new adventure. Sometimes I waited in bed, listening for any stirring in the house. Was the little ball of energy up and ready to roll yet?

In no time, Alex's smiling face would peek around the corner with his short spiky hair sticking up in all directions. *Bright-eyed and bushy-tailed*, he would scramble straight to my bedside with a big hug.

"Good morning, Mommy!" were the first words out of his mouth.

"Good morning, world!" That was an expression my Mother used to say as she greeted a new day. I grabbed one more little snuggle before throwing off the covers and springing out of bed.

Alex bounded to his bedroom. "I'll wear this. No, this," he said cheerily as he threw open the dresser drawers, pulling out one thing after another. With determination, he laid his top choices for the day across his bed.

"These are my favorites," he pronounced, waving his camouflaged pants with the belts and loops; they were his regular choice.

He decorated his waist with things little boys enjoy: a compass, a flash light, and a Swiss army knife. He then finished off the outfit with a little sack of bobbers and hooks dangling at his side. I could hear the gadgets clanging as he made his way out the back door.

Following him outside, I found him sitting on the steps, pulling on his favorite black rubber boots still caked with mud from our last adventure.

"What a beautiful day it's going to be," I pointed out, imagining what idea might be on Alex's busy mind.

Our cane poles with red and white bobbers were calling out to us, hanging on hooks overhead in the carport in clear view. They were not fancy fishing poles, but they were special to us. We bought them on our church camping trip.

Alex turned and looked at the poles, and then looked slowly back at me. His little grin preceded his question, "Can we go fishing?"

I did not have to think twice before saying, "I'd love to go fishing with you, Son. But first, let's do our morning devotions."

Our scripture for the day was Psalm 91:11, "For he will command his angels concerning you to guard you in all your ways." After we said our prayers, we packed our gear and off we went to one of our favorite fishing spots.

"Let's catch a whole bucket of fish today, Mom."

"Okay, that's a great idea, Alex. Let's go!"

It was a beautiful scenic drive to the park where we often fished. There was a playground by the lake, and we rarely passed by without stopping for a turn on the monkey bars and swing set.

"Mom, I think I have the wiggles again," said Alex, wanting to get rid of some of the pent-up energy that little boys naturally have. After a few whirls and twirls and a slip down the slide, we were ready to get focused on our fishing plans.

"Now, let's tackle the tackle," he said with a giggle. With our gear in tow, we crossed the grassy field and staked our claim in a shady location for the morning.

The water was already alive with a few small fishing boats and a ski boat skimming along, towing its skier effortlessly. The lake looked so inviting with the hot morning sun reflecting on the cool water. I loved our uninterrupted time together when we really did not have anything to do except make sure there was a bobber and a worm on the line.

I had just begun to set up our spot when I heard a scream, "Mommy, Mommy! Hurry, come and help me!"

I quickly turned to see why he was shouting when I saw Alex jumping into the water. He was splashing and screaming, swatting his arms and legs, crying uncontrollably. All that I could see was a cloud of small bugs flying around him. Without hesitation, I threw my things to the ground, ran as fast as I could, and grabbed him from the water's edge.

"Stay calm, it's alright, I'm right here." Pulling him out of the water, I strained to see what the matter was. I needed to get him away from the immediate danger. Quickly taking Alex over to the blanket, I set him down, trying to see what had happened to him. It looked like we had disturbed a nearby wasp nest.

"Calm down now, and take a deep breath," I told him as I tried to catch my own as well. Alex sat on the blanket while I examined him. His arms and legs were covered with bites.

James 5:13 instantly came to my mind: "Is anyone of you in trouble? He should pray." I said this verse over and over to myself as I silently cried out to the Lord, asking him for guidance for the next few steps. I tried to hide my fear from Alex so that I could calm him down.

Out of the corner of my eye, I saw a small woman with a rolled up newspaper in her hand quickly approaching us. Before now, I had not seen anyone near our spot by the lake. She seemed to have come out of nowhere. With a soft voice, she whispered, "It's going to be alright." She gently placed her hand on my shoulder. "Be careful, step aside," she said as she stood between us, swatting at the yellow jackets that were still swarming nearby.

"Oh, you're a godsend," I said with relief. It was surprising how this brave, little lady was able to get rid of the dangerous, stinging insects so quickly. In just a matter of seconds, the bugs had disappeared—there was not a single bug in sight.

Once there were no more signs of the painful bugs, the kind woman came over and sat beside us, making sure we were okay. "May I pray for you?" she asked in a whisper. Alex and I looked at each other with a sigh of relief. We were more than glad to hear the comforting words of a prayer.

"Dear Lord, thank you for rescuing this boy from danger. We thank you for being faithful in our time of need. Please protect us from getting any more stings. In Jesus' name, Amen."

Her calm, soothing voice was a comfort to us both. Alex's sniffles soon vanished, and my dampened eyes soon dried, too. "I live right around the corner," our new friend told us. "I just happened to walk to the park to read my newspaper today." Her warm smile assured us that she was glad to meet us that day and lend her assistance.

"We're thankful to the Lord for you and that you were here just in the *nick of time*. Thank you for praying and comforting us," I told her, clasping her hands. I was grateful that Alex could see how we had been blessed, and how our powerful God watches out for us at all times.

"He is always with us," said our rescuer. She stayed with us a short time and talked with us about the Lord's goodness and faithfulness, and then went on her way. We never saw her again after that day, and we regretted that we never got her name.

"God sent that kind woman to help us," I told Alex as we reflected on our devotions from that morning. "Thank you, Lord, for going before us and providing just what we needed in our desperate moment," I prayed.

"That kind lady reminds me of an angel," Alex remarked. "Even though the fish didn't bite today, Mommy, we were surely blessed from the bites we did get—blessed by the prayers of the sweet lady." She left an unforgettable impression of God's kindness on both of us.

"That's right, Alex," I said, watching him scratch his stings. "God is always with us, and He always hears our prayers."

Yellow jackets are a type of wasp with a bold, aggressive sting and are particularly attracted to the water. Yellow jacket nests can grow to the size of a basketball and are found in trees and shrubs. They are frequent invaders of picnics. Their sting is painful, but it is only poisonous to those who are allergic.

Discussion

How does having morning devotions help you throughout the day? What do you look forward to on Saturday mornings? What sure thing can we do in our time of need? Can you remember a time when God came to your rescue in a surprising way? What is one way to show appreciation when someone helps you?

Scripture

"But those who suffer he delivers in their suffering; he speaks to them in their affliction." Job 36:15

"The angel of the Lord encamps around those who fear him, and he delivers them." Psalm 34:7

"But when the kindness and love of God our Savior appeared, he saved us, not because of righteous things we had done, but because of his mercy." Titus 3:4–5

Song

"All Night, All Day (Angels Watching Over Me)" and "I Need Thee Every Hour"

Application

Visit your favorite playground for a picnic. Claim a favorite fishing hole and cast your hook, line, bobber, and pole. Use colored glue to decorate a plastic beach bucket or tackle box with your name or favorite scripture. Surprise your Mom and clean the mud off your boots.

Idiom

Bright-eyed and bushy-tailed means full of energy usually referring to early morning.
Nick of time means at the last possible moment.

Prayer

Thank the Lord for watching over you and for rescuing you in your time of trouble.

Chapter 14

The Great Wait

"Rejoice with those who rejoice;
mourn with those who mourn."

ROMANS 12:15

From the time Alex could say the word "doggie," he wanted a dog. Like most parents, my first inclination was to get him one. I told a friend of mine who was a veterinarian assistant that Alex really wanted a dog.

"Children are much better with dogs if they wait until at least age ten," he cautioned. He told me this was the age he had seen the greatest success with children caring for animals. Despite his advice, waiting was still a real challenge when I thought of all the reasons why we should get a dog.

A year before Alex turned ten, we went for a Saturday walk in our neighborhood taking our usual route. The early morning sun was peeking through the trees as Alex rode his bike and I walked.

I recalled a favorite scripture encouraging parents to make the most of moments such as these. This was one of those cherished opportunities when we were not distracted and we could talk. The subject of getting a dog came up again that day.

"Mom, why do we have to wait so long to get a dog? I think I'm big enough now," Alex pleaded.

"The Lord is our Father," I assured him. "He'll surely show us just the right time to get a dog, but until then we have to be patient and wait."

On our way home, we noticed a little dog following us. "Mom, look at the cute little doggie," Alex was excited to inform me.

"He is a cute dog, Alex. I hope he's not lost," I whispered. The bristly-haired dog looked like he could use a bath pronto.

"I just want to snatch him up and take him home with us," said Alex with longing eyes.

"Alex, I don't think we should do that," I answered. "His family will be sad when they find he's missing." It was difficult for Alex to keep his hands off the cute little pup. *Could he be thinking about rescuing this dog?* I wondered.

We were not ready for a pet because of our busy schedule; a dog would be stretching our family even more. The Bible says to listen to those who have gone before us. The Lord often uses the experience and expertise of other people to teach and direct us. We had been given good advice, and I believed that this was the perfect opportunity to put it into practice.

We trusted that our veterinary friend knew what he was talking about. The heartbreak of having a dog, not being able to properly care for it, and eventually having to give it up seemed worse than having to wait until the right time.

The clanging of dog tags kept us looking back at our new little friend who was following close behind us, wagging his tail in short, snappy jerks. Alex was captivated by every move the little dog made.

"Come on Alex. Let's walk a little faster and maybe he'll turn around and go back to his home," I said. I did not want to lead the dog out of his neighborhood.

The expression on Alex's face showed that it took every muscle in his frame to keep walking with his gaze straight ahead. His anxious body wanted to turn around and pick up the pup that by now was as close as a shadow.

We arrived back home with the dog still following close behind. "I think it's best if we leave him outside," I told Alex. *Surely he'll find his way home sooner or later*, I thought.

"I'll get him some water," Alex said, holding the water hose. I went inside and called the phone number on the dog tags, but no one answered. Sitting by the window that afternoon, I watched Alex as he played in the yard with the dog. We were waiting to see if someone in the neighborhood might drive by and recognize him.

"Mom, he's so cute!" Alex insisted as he played with the friendly pup. I knew Alex was hoping that we were going to keep the dog. It was obvious he had his *heart set on it*. We were able to enjoy the dog that day, even though he did not belong to us.

As the afternoon merged into the evening, I decided I should try once more to locate the dog's owner. When I finally reached the owners and told them, "I think we have your dog," they were very relieved. Soon a car drove up and a brother and sister got out and came running.

"Here, Buddy," they called for him. The reunion was so sweet as the little pup wagged his tail and jumped up and down all over his owners. Although Alex was disappointed to say goodbye to Buddy, he was happy that their family was reunited.

I consoled Alex later after commending him for honoring me with his good attitude. "Sometimes we have to wait for the things we want. Releasing the dog to its owner is like releasing our desires to our Heavenly Father and trusting that He knows what is best for us."

After discussing the day's events, Alex prayed. "Dear Heavenly Father, thank you for the chance to play with Buddy today, and helping us find his owners. May I still please have a dog someday, if it's your will? Amen."

The simple circumstances God allows us to experience with our children can be valuable character building moments. The following year, when Alex turned ten years old, our veterinarian friend gave us the most wonderful dog we could have ever imagined. Penny became part of our family, and we had many years of happy memories with her.

Alex still reminds me today that having to wait to get his own dog made him appreciate Penny so much more. Sometimes "no" can mean "not this one" or "not at this time." But even more importantly, the word "wait" can end up being "great."

"Love the Lord your God with all your heart and with all your soul and with all your strength. These commandments that I give you today are to be upon your hearts. Impress them on your children. Talk about them when you sit at home and when you walk along the road, when you lie down and when you get up." Deuteronomy 6:5–7

Discussion

Why is timing so important when owning a pet? Why would it be wise to seek the advice of "experts" before getting a pet? Why is learning to wait on the Lord necessary to becoming a mature Christian? What does the phrase "wait can end up being great" mean? How can we bless the Lord when things do not go our way? Why does God want us to rejoice for others?

Scripture

"In the morning, O Lord, you hear my voice; in the morning I lay my requests before you and wait in expectation." Psalm 5:3

"Yet the LORD longs to be gracious to you; he rises to show you compassion. For the Lord is a God of justice. Blessed are all who wait for him!" Isaiah 30:18

"But those who hope in the Lord will renew their strength. They will soar on wings like eagles; they will run and not grow weary, they will walk and not be faint." Isaiah 40:31

Song

"Do Lord, Do Lord (Do Remember Me)" and "Rejoice In The Lord Always (Again I Say Rejoice)"

Application

Consider doing "pet sitting" in your church or neighborhood. Include walking, feeding, or grooming pets. Take your pet to visit someone who is lonely. Allow them to enjoy the companionship of your cherished friend Make a colorful animal decoupage from cut outs of magazines. Sketch a picture of you "being patient" and explain what you have drawn.

Idiom

Heart set on it means to want something very much.

Prayer

Thank the Lord with a grateful heart for the privilege of owning a pet. or, if you don't have your own, rejoice with someone who lets you play with their pet.

Chapter 15

Paper Mache, Olé!

"This is the day the LORD has made;
let us rejoice and be glad in it."

Psalm 118:24

Alex was sitting at the kitchen table, looking at the calendar. His tenth birthday was right around the corner and he was counting down the days. Every night, before he went to bed, he marked another X on the next day of the month. He was especially looking forward to his big "double-digit" birthday, so I wanted it to be a special day.

"Mom, can I have a piñata for my birthday?"

"Let's pray about it and see what the Lord provides," I answered. I shopped around, looking for a basketball piñata because, at the time, basketball was Alex's favorite sport. Not only was a piñata not in my budget, but it seemed difficult to find one at any price. The searching and waiting for the piñata began.

"Mom, only two more weeks until my birthday," Alex walked by and whispered as I talked on the phone with my friend Joy one day.

"I haven't forgotten, Alex, and neither has the Lord," I whispered back.

Joy told me about the time she had made a piñata for one of her children and how much they loved it. "Let's make one for Alex over here at my house," she offered. Hope sprung up anew! We planned to get together and give it a try.

For the next couple of weeks, we went to Joy's house in the mornings, before I went to work, and began working on a piñata. Alex, Joy's four children, and I were spread out across the living room floor. We were surrounded by stacks of newspapers, torn into thin strips, and tin pans almost overflowing with sticky white flour paste.

"You're all doing a beautiful job," I told the busy sculptors. We had glue and paper stuck to our fingers, as well as between our toes, as we worked our way around and through the big mess.

"What's it going to be?" Alex asked.

"It's a surprise!" the whole design team exclaimed with a shout. We tried hard to keep the identity a secret. Finally, a crinkled and wrinkled, round blob emerged that looked like a large shriveled prune. The children had a lot of fun working with the paper and messy glue, and enjoyed keeping the secret from Alex.

"That's incredible, Mom! What do we call it?" asked Alex with glee.

"Let's just call it a birthday ball," I laughed, still being secretive. I turned to Joy and said, "I can't believe what fun this is, and how you've made it all possible. Thank you, thank you!"

Carrying it carefully outside, we decorated the "blob" with fluorescent orange paint and black stripes, completing the masterpiece. As Alex watched everyone putting together the shape and the colors, he suddenly realized what it was.

"A basketball!" he squealed. He ran to Joy and gave her a big hug.

"Happy Birthday, Alex! Paper mache, olé!" The children cheered and clapped together as we walked to the back yard. "Paper mache, olé! Paper mache, olé!" they chanted, in unison like a cheering squad.

We gathered together outside, and hung the prize basketball piñata out on the clothesline to dry. We huddled around the bright orange ball, carefully inspecting it to make sure every piece was tightly glued. The children were overjoyed to see their project successfully completed.

Alex invited eight of his friends to his birthday party the following Friday. It was a beautiful, cool, autumn night—perfect evening for a party. After pizza and cake, we made our way outside to the carport and strung a rope on the overhead rafters of the roof.

"I want to be first," were the words that echoed from all directions. We carefully tied the large orange globe to the rope, and pulled it up slowly, making sure it did not come apart. Hands and fingers reached upward with more pleadings.

"I want to be first, me first!" the children shouted.

There it hung, the lop-sided but beloved sculpture. It felt like we had just erected the most spectacular birthday monument ever. At first, the bright orange ball seemed a little shaky, but after a few tugs on the rope we found it to be ready and steady. The piñata was packed to the brim with gum, candy, and lots of fun little surprises.

"Go, Birthday Boy!" the crowd shouted as Alex stepped up to bat first and whacked away. He swung swiftly and deliberately as the candy trickled out to the ground with each hard blow. The children murmured excitedly wondering who would deal the final whack.

The children lined up, were blindfolded, and one by one took turns at bat with the broomstick. The onlookers waiting in line cheered like it was a live basketball game. We wanted everyone to get a chance, and they did, each one, with three swings.

Michelle, the strongest and oldest girl, was next in line. She wound up, swung hard, and landed the final blow as the crowd cheered, "Go, Shelly, go!" Candy flew to every corner of the carport. The children scrambled like *chickens on a June bug* and scooped up the sweet treasures into their mouths, hands, and pockets. The main event was over. Our piñata was a huge success, and our hearts were full.

Alex and the children enjoyed the entire project and had a wonderful party. A few days later, I received a phone call from a mother of one of the children who came to the party. She was also a single mother like me.

"I don't have money to have a birthday party for my son," she confided. I was able to share with her how God had provided for us. She told me she was encouraged and talked about how much fun her son had had at the party.

The true success of the party was being able to rejoice in the goodness of the Lord, and how He provided everything for Alex's birthday. The Lord delights in His children and wants to bless us and give us good things to share with others.

"The LORD your God is with you, he is mighty to save. He will take great delight in you, he will quiet you with his love, he will rejoice over you with singing." Zephaniah 3:17

Discussion

What is your most cherished birthday memory? What birthday gift have you received for which you are most grateful? What is your favorite food to eat on your birthday? How did the two families' joint effort make the party a success? What is one way you can celebrate the love of Jesus every day of the year?

Scripture

"Surely goodness and love will follow me all the days of my life, and I will dwell in the house of the Lord, forever." Psalm 23:6

"But may the righteous be glad and rejoice before God; may they be happy and joyful." Psalm 68:3

"I will praise God's name in song and glorify him with thanksgiving." Psalm 69:30

"His children will be mighty in the land; the generation of the upright will be blessed." Psalm 112:2

Song

"God Is So Good" and "This Is The Day That The Lord Has Made"

Application

Birthdays are personal and original traditions. Throw a surprise party for someone to encourage them. Personalize the party specifically for that individual and serve their favorite food. Bake a cake to match the theme of the party. Make a budget for the party, and stick to it. Plan your own paper mache project with a small group. Make noise makers using cans, beans, and coins.

Idiom

Chicken on a June bug means eagerly, and totally, on or after something.

Prayer

Ask the Lord to lead you to someone who you can bless. Thank God for the gift of His son Jesus.

Chapter 16

The Doorkeeper

*"Enter his gates with thanksgiving and his courts
with praise; give thanks to him and praise his name."*

PSALM 100:4

Sunday was our favorite day of the week, and what a welcomed day of rest it was. The smell of freshly baked cinnamon rolls filled the morning air. Soon, with our tummies full and our best clothes on, we were well on our way to joining our fellow believers at church.

Getting out the door on time was often our only obstacle. Many times the hectic week left us in a slow and laid-back pace. Regretfully, arriving a few minutes late for church was not uncommon for us.

The easy-going, casual approach to this Sunday morning's routine stopped at the steps of our church. At the front door, handing out programs stood the chief doorkeeper. Well, that is what we called him. He was our friend Mr. Chuck, who welcomed each person who walked through the doors.

Unfortunately, we were late again today. When we approached Mr. Chuck, he was pulling back the sleeve of his jacket, checking his watch. "Hello, Lynn. Good morning, Alex," he said, rubbing Alex's head as we walked by.

"Good morning to you, Mr. Chuck," I said right back as he handed me the morning's program. The word "late" was never spoken.

This same scene kept repeating itself each week. "Mom, we're going to be late again," Alex reminded me as we approached the church parking lot. I could see that our tardiness was starting to bother him as much as it bothered me.

"Sorry, Hun, I'll work on it." I knew it would be a challenge to leave for church sooner. I would have to make adjustments to our schedule. I enjoyed our entire Sunday morning ritual—sleeping in a little later and the smell of cinnamon rolls in the oven. I could not ask for more.

This pattern of being late for church continued. It went something like this. We were late, Mr. Chuck checked his watched, he smiled, and then handed us a bulletin. He never had to speak a word and was never rude or unkind—always a perfectly warm and welcoming gentleman.

I was the one who was disappointed with myself for not being diligent about my punctuality. The time-watching began to speak its own message to me. The conviction I felt was beginning to motivate me to change.

Mr. Chuck always had a big grin on his face. I do not think I ever saw him without it, but sometimes his gentle weekly prodding letting me know that we were late irritated me.

Over time, God used Mr. Chuck's faithfulness to change my heart and mind. One Saturday evening, I felt inspired by the Lord to take the issue of getting to church on time more seriously. After all, I was never late to work or a basketball game.

"Okay, Alex, it's time to go to bed."

"Mom, why are we going to bed so early?" asked Alex, surprised that we had changed our Saturday evening routine.

"Well, Alex, the Lord has impressed on my heart that we need to make every effort to get to church on time, and I want to begin tomorrow. Let's do all we can to greet Mr. Chuck before church starts."

"Let's do it, Mom. Give me a five!"

"Alright, Alex, let's do it. *The early bird gets the worm!*" With a high five, we sealed our plan.

Setting the alarm earlier was the first part of our strategy. Determined to improve our punctuality, I even set the breakfast table the night before. I carefully made sure our clothes were pressed and laid out, every stitch and crease in its proper place. After tucking Alex in as *snug as a bug in a rug*, "Good night, sweet dreams," and "I love you," were my final words of the night.

"I love you, too," Alex echoed back.

Early the next morning, I felt a gentle tug on my blanket. "Mommy, it's time to get up."

"Did the alarm go off already?" I rolled over and asked.

"No, Ma'am, but the sun is up." Jumping to my feet, I embraced the day with a joyful heart. Without giving up any part of our cherished Sunday morning tradition, we left the house on time that morning, arriving at the church earlier than usual.

We stepped up our pace a notch as we walked through the parking lot to the front door. Mr. Chuck glanced once—then again—and realized that it was us coming up the walkway. A grin spread across his face as if it was the first time we had met. "Well, howdy, ya'll; what a nice surprise!"

"Good morning, Mr. Chuck," said Alex. We were both proud and pleased that we made it on time. The greatest part was standing there beside Mr. Chuck as he passed out the bulletins. We were happy to help him greet the rest of our church family.

"Mommy, that was so much fun getting to church early today," Alex told me on our way home. My eyes were opened that day to the blessings we received from those few extra minutes before church. Mr. Chuck's greeting this morning felt like a benediction.

"I must confess something, Alex. There was a time when Mr. Chuck annoyed me, checking his watch each week. But now, I am so grateful to the Lord for using him to teach us about punctuality. God's house is the best place to be on time." The accountability of Mr. Chuck was no longer a bother to me, but a warm and welcoming reminder.

Getting to church on time, or even early, is a priority to us today. This new outlook is a result of the care of Mr. Chuck, the doorkeeper. Although words never crossed between him and us about our being late, we were grateful for his faithful eye on the clock.

Mr. Chuck is still the doorkeeper at his church today. When we visit Florida, we try to get to church early so we can surprise him and stand at the door and talk with him. We are blessed to have known Mr. Chuck and his family for over seventeen years. They remain our dear friends today.

"And do this, understanding the present time. The hour has come for you to wake up from your slumber, because our salvation is nearer now than when we first believed." Romans 13:11

Discussion

What is one of your family's meaningful Sunday traditions? What are some blessings of being punctual for church? What could you do to help your family get to church on time? Why is it so important to have Christian fellowship? What is your favorite food to eat for breakfast on Sunday mornings?

From the Bible

"Better is one day in your courts than a thousand elsewhere; I would rather be a doorkeeper in the house of my God than dwell in the tents of the wicked." Psalm 84:10

"There is a time for everything, and a season for every activity under heaven." Ecclesiastes 3:1

"Let us not give up meeting together, as some are in the habit of doing, but let us encourage one another—and all the more as you see the Day approaching." Hebrews 10:25

Song

"There's A Sweet, Sweet Spirit In This Place" and "I Worship You O Mighty God"

Application

Hold others accountable for being on time, but do it with a smile. Make a card for your church doorkeeper or pastor to show your appreciation for their service to your church family. Wake up a little earlier on Sunday morning, and help a sibling get ready for church. Set the table on Saturday night in preparation for Sunday morning breakfast.

Idiom

The early bird gets the worm means it is beneficial to plan ahead.
Snug as a bug in a rug means comfortable and cozy in your bed.

Prayer

Thank God for your church and the people who give their time to serve. Ask Him to show you where you can give your time to do His Kingdom work.

Chapter 17

The Unchecked Blank

*"In my Father's house are many rooms; if
it were not so, I would have told you. I am
going there to prepare a place for you."*

JOHN 14:2

"Everyone come in and have a seat," said Mr. Pent. He directed us to come inside, greeting us with a big smile. Mr. Pent was the elder leading our church's first mission trip. "We're so excited for this opportunity to go to Mexico. Let's divide into groups and make plans for VBS."

The crowd quickly filed into the meeting room, and the group split into two. This was the first meeting to plan our mission trip across the border. A sign-up sheet was passed around, listing all the materials that were needed for Vacation Bible School.

"There are a few more items on the list that are unchecked," Mr. Pent pointed out. When the list went around the room once more, there was one blank left unchecked. This unchecked blank would later become instrumental in revealing the providence of God for our family.

"Okay, we have everything checked off the list, except one more thing that we need. Who wants to volunteer to find a felt board for the VBS? We can't do VBS without it!" Scanning the group, he looked expectantly for a volunteer. Waving the white piece of paper in the air for all to see Mr. Pent walked over to our group.

"The felt board is very important. We need it for the Bible lessons."

"I know where to get a felt board!" Whitney exclaimed, raising her hand enthusiastically.

"Thank you, Whitney. We can check this off our list now," he replied.

The following week, Alex and I went with Whitney to find a felt board for the mission trip. We drove to the ministry house where she had attended a missions training camp the previous summer. A tall, gray-haired man greeted us at the door.

"Hello, Mr. Humphrey. Do you remember me?" Whitney smiled and asked.

"Well, I believe I taught you here during last summer's training session for Vacation Bible School. Am I right?"

"Yes, Sir, you remember! I'm Whitney. It's good to see you again. These are my friends Miss Lynn and Alex."

"It's nice to meet you," Mr. Humphrey replied. "What brings you here today?"

Whitney explained, "Our church is planning a mission trip to Mexico, so we came to see if you have any more of those blue felt boards."

"Oh, how wonderful! I have just what you're looking for." Mr. Humphrey did not have to think twice about it. He turned and walked over to a closet, where the felt boards were stored.

"Here you go, Whitney." Mr. Humphrey handed Whitney a large, soft, bright blue felt board. Suddenly, my mind was awakened with the memories of when I was a little girl around age seven. That was the first time I remember hearing about Jesus.

"Mr. Humphrey, I remember seeing a blue felt board like this one when I was a little girl. There was a lady that came to the project where I lived and told Bible stories to the children there every Saturday morning." As I shared this memory with him, it felt like it was just yesterday.

"Where did you live when you were a little girl, Miss Lynn?" he kindly asked.

"I lived in the housing project over on South Street." The look on his face changed from courtesy to curiosity as he listened intently.

"The Bible teacher came every Saturday, but I never knew her name. I never missed going, because at the end of the Bible lesson she gave each of us a piece of ribbon candy."

"If my math is correct that was over thirty years ago." Mr. Humphrey eyes filled with tears. "I remember who the sweet little lady was, who taught the Bible over there where you lived."

My heart raced as I waited to hear what this kind gentleman was getting ready to say. "That lady was Edith Wells. She had a *heart of gold*." Tears rolled down his face as he spoke.

"Edith Wells came right here to get that blue felt board. Right here, in this very place!" he exclaimed. "She came in here week after week to buy supplies for the Backyard Bible School in that project. She was often very discouraged when she came. Week after week, she wondered if any of the children were listening to her share about Jesus."

Mr. Humphrey was as thrilled as I was to realize the fruit of Edith Wells' commitment. This was the first time in my life that I had ever heard of someone who had gone before me, for my sake—for my faith.

Mr. Humphrey continued, "I used to tell her, 'Edith, you just keep telling them about Jesus. Nothing you do for Him will be wasted.'"

By now, I also had tears in my eyes as I realized that this was the lady that gave me the ribbon candy when I was a young child. This was the lady with the blue felt board. She was the dear soul that first told me about Jesus.

"Now, here you are to buy a blue felt board so that you, your son, and your church can tell others about Jesus, too!" We were all reaching for the Kleenex box by now, wiping away our tears of joy.

"Edith never realized the fruit of her labor when she was alive. But now, she is rejoicing in Heaven knowing that you know Jesus!" We were all *taken back* by this revelation. It was a very somber moment for me, as I realized that another Christian loved me enough to teach me about Jesus.

We left the office of Mr. Humphrey that day with a new appreciation for people that invest their time teaching the Bible. I never forgot those days when I was a child at the courtyard, listening to the Bible stories. Today, the images of a figure of Jesus on a blue felt board live in my heart and remind me that I am never alone.

Whitney, Alex, and I were more energized than before to prepare for the trip to Mexico. I now knew the meaning of the unchecked blank on the list that day at church—the now-checked blank. It revealed how God prepared the way for me to hear His Word. Edith Wells met a need in my heart as a child, a need I did not realize, and one she unknowingly filled.

I thank the Lord for the love and devotion of Edith Wells and for Mr. Humphrey for supplying our team with our blue felt board. We left that day ready to plan for our mission trip with our own story to tell.

"Many, O Lord my God, are the wonders you have done. The things you planned for us no one can recount to you; were I to speak and tell of them, they would be too many to declare." Psalm 40:5

Discussion

Tell the story of when you first heard about Jesus. Why was the "unchecked blank" so significant in revealing God's providence? Why is faith so necessary for a servant of the Lord? Why is commitment vital to see the fruit of your labor?

Scripture

"Your statutes are my heritage forever; they are the joy of my heart." Psalm 119:111

"Train a child in the way he should go, and when he is old he will not turn from it." Proverbs 22:6

"For I know the plans I have for you," declares the LORD, "plans to prosper you and not to harm you, plans to give you hope and a future." Jeremiah 29:11

Song

"When The Roll Is Called Up Yonder" and "Thank You Lord For Saving My Soul"

Application

Share the hope of your family vision. Tell the story of when you made the decision to accept Christ. Parents, tell why someone you admire is a Godly influence in your life (e.g., parent, pastor, mentor). Make a blue felt board out of cardboard, felt, and tape. Draw Bible characters on pieces of paper, and glue them to the scraps of felt. Use your new felt board to host a Backyard Bible School. Invite neighbors, friends, and family.

Idiom

Taken back means awestruck by an unexpected circumstance.
Heart of gold means extremely kind.

Prayer

Ask the Lord to bless His missionaries around the world.

Chapter 18

Labels

*"I can do everything through him
who gives me strength."*

<small>PHILIPPIANS 4:13</small>

It was late when I finished work most days. I was a "domestic engineer" in the Orlando area, the town where I grew up. That is a fancy way of saying that I cleaned houses. I was grateful for my work, because it allowed me to be a full-time mother. Alex went to work with me most days. At the end of each day, we were glad to get home for some rest and refueling.

"Alex, please come in here while I cook dinner and you can read to me." Sitting on the kitchen floor, he read his school books to me while I prepared the evening meal. I always welcomed a chance to encourage Alex as he learned.

"Mom, what's this word?" he would ask with each page he turned. I would switch back and forth between sounding out words and meal preparations. "Mom, I can't read," Alex often repeated in frustration.

"Alex, you are learning to read. Be patient with yourself. I know you can do it." In my heart, I knew that sooner or later he would learn to read. Comparing ourselves to others seemed unproductive as did "labeling" ourselves according to others' standards. With God's help, Alex would learn to read in his own time; that was my prayer.

Each day offered unique challenges and opportunities to learn something new. My mind was constantly churning, thinking of new ways to make reading fun. One day after work, I decided to try something different as I sat down to read with him.

"Alex, would you get a can of soup out of the cabinet for me, please?" I asked, entering the meal preparation mode. He handed me the can of soup, and I handed it right back to him saying, "Why don't you read everything that's on that label to me while I'm cooking."

"Okay, Mom. I'll give it a try." Syllable by syllable he began to sound out the words. We patiently read through the instructions and ingredients on the label, both benefiting from the interaction. My cozy kitchen was transformed into a schoolroom.

Each afternoon Alex reached for a new item from the pantry. There was progress in the Hurtado Homeschool. Little by little, I saw Alex having fun, learning to read by having words presented to him in a unique way.

After grocery shopping one day, Alex surprised me. "Mom, where's your receipt from the store? I want to check the groceries." I gave him the sales receipt, not sure what he was going to do next.

"Alex, what are you going to do?" I questioned.

"Look, Mom, this is so easy. I just look at the name on the label and then try to match it on the receipt." I was thrilled as I watched him unpack, stack, and match each item from the store. His confidence increased as he was able to recognize all of the words on the labels. It was a blessing to see that he was making progress with his reading.

One particular day, Alex went to work with me. "Come on, it's time to go to work. Don't forget your school books," I instructed.

We drove to south Orlando to clean my friend Suzy's house. Alex loved to go to her house because he liked to play with her dog Ginger. Ginger enjoyed playing with Alex, too.

After a game of catch-n-fetch in the backyard, Alex took a seat at the dining room table to study. When I went to the back of the house to start cleaning, I realized I had left my things at the front door. I summoned Alex to *give me a hand*. "Alex, would you please bring me the cleaning supplies?"

I was working in the back bathroom, rinsing out the shower, when I heard him call, "Mom!" He stood behind me, holding a white plastic bottle. He was slowly sounding out the words on the label, "Mil-dew re-mo-ver." He said it again, several times. "Mom, I did it. I can read it. It says 'mil-dew re-mo-ver.' Is that right, Mom?"

"Yes, that's right, you did it! You can read it," I cheered.

"Mom, I can read, I read this label all by myself!" The expression on his face caused my *heart to skip a beat*. He stood there in the bathroom and read some of the other labels to me. The ride home that day was exhilarating. Alex tried to read all the road signs he saw on the way.

"I can read, Mom. I can do it. Praise the Lord, I can read!"

"Yes you can, Alex. Your perseverance has really paid off!"

What a transformation from months ago, I thought to myself. *Now he's reading to me.* His reading continued to improve as he applied himself every day. We labeled this as one of our happiest homeschooling memories.

I was not as concerned about his reading after that day as I saw the fruit of simple efforts. As Alex became a better reader, it sparked his interest to learn other things as well. There was still a long way to go, but he was well on his way. The prayer of my heart was answered as Alex became increasingly motivated and willing to learn.

Reading labels was just one creative way Alex found helpful while learning to read. The added time we spent together was another extra blessing. He eventually became an excellent reader. That school year, Alex made labels for his notebooks that read, "I can do everything through him who gives me strength. Philippians 4:13." This was our reminder that God is the source of our strength and inspiration.

"But encourage one another daily, as long as it is called Today, so that none of you may be hardened by sin's deceitfulness." Hebrews 3:13

Discussion

What are some ways you can encourage yourself in the Lord? How does confidence in the Lord help you overcome difficulties? Are you most encouraged by words or deeds? Give one example. What is the harm of comparing ourselves with others? What simple steps can you take to improve your reading abilities?

Scripture

"but David encouraged himself in the LORD his God."
1 Samuel 30:6b (KJV)

"But blessed is the man who trusts in the Lord, whose confidence is in him." Jeremiah 17:7

"We do not dare to classify or compare ourselves with some who commend themselves. When they measure themselves by themselves and compare themselves with themselves, they are not wise."
2 Corinthians 10:12

Song

"He's Still Working On Me" and "He Is Able"

Application

Turn your kitchen or living area into a mini-mart. Watch your child's confidence soar as they play grocery store. Let your child assist you in making a grocery list from the newspaper ads. Set up a devotion schedule so that everyone can take a turn reading to the family. Practice reading with your child by reading road signs while you are in the car. Parents, reward baby steps on the way to mastering a new skill.

Idiom

Heart to skip a beat means a sudden or excited response.
Give me a hand means to help with a minimal task.

Prayer

Ask the Lord to help you persevere through any difficult challenges you are facing. Thank Him for His faithfulness.

Chapter 19

Secret Pal

"I thank my God every time I remember you."

PHILIPPIANS 1:3

"Let's celebrate! It's Wednesday, and we're halfway through the week. Let's do something fun today that will encourage and bless someone." Alex was all smiles at my suggestion. He loved anything that distracted from the humdrum routine. We both did.

It was the end of the month, and we had to go to the homeschool office after work to drop off our school reports. "I have an idea, Alex. But, it's a surprise!"

"What, Mom?" His eyes sparkled with excitement. By then, I had pulled into the grocery store parking lot.

"Why are we stopping here?" he asked.

"I need to get a gift," I answered. We headed into the store, and went straight to the flower department.

"Who are you buying flowers for, Mother?"

"Well, let's just say it's for someone really special. I'll explain when we get in the car." We walked through the card aisle on the way to check out, and the words "secret pal" on one of the cards *caught my eye. What a great idea*, I thought. So I bought the most beautiful "secret pal" card that there was.

By now I had already forgotten the monotonous routine that we were trying to escape. "Alex, these flowers are for our special friend, Miss Marie."

Miss Marie is someone near and dear to our hearts. She worked at the homeschool office and had mentored us since the beginning of our homeschool journey. She was our brightest cheerleader. When I think of her, the words "With God, all things are possible" come to mind.

"We're going to give the flowers to her with this secret pal card," I said.

"But then it won't be a secret if we give them to her," Alex quipped.

"Sure, it will. We're going to leave them at her door. We'll be the secret. A secret pal is someone who secretly blesses another person for whom they are thankful. You do things for them without letting them know it's you. We have fun doing the blessing, and they have fun doing the guessing."

"Goodie! She's going to be so surprised," Alex bubbled with excitement. We sat in the car and signed the card before going upstairs to deliver the bright yellow sunflowers.

It read, "To Miss Marie: With lots of love, from your two secret pals."

We first submitted the school reports and then went down the hall to leave the vase of flowers and card at Miss Marie's office door. How long could we keep our identity hidden?

We giggled all the way down the stairs as we left her office. "She'll never guess it was us," Alex chuckled. After we arrived home that day, Alex told me over and over how much he enjoyed delivering the bouquet of sunshine to our special friend.

"Alex, I believe the reason we enjoyed it so much was because we were thinking about someone else. We can get discouraged and ungrateful when we're always thinking about ourselves."

Soon the next month rolled around, and school reports were due again. Alex had already thought ahead. "Mom, let's take Miss Marie another surprise."

"Oh, you remembered," I said with delight. He went into his room and brought out a ceramic dish of a little boy with his dog.

"Let's give this to Miss Marie for her office."

"What a wonderful idea, Alex. She'll love it."

Alex wrapped the dish and attached a card that he had made. We left the small package at the door of Miss Marie's office, hoping that it would bring her joy and brighten her day.

"Having a secret pal is really fun," Alex said as we drove home.

"Yes, it is," I agreed. "I didn't even think about it being Wednesday today."

"Mom, I have another idea. Let's declare Wednesday 'Secret Pal Day.'"

"That's a great idea!" I nodded and whole-heartedly agreed.

We continued making secret visits to our special friend, leaving trinkets and notes at her office door. The end of the school year was right around the corner, and we would not be seeing her over the summer break. The time had come to reveal our identity to our friend. One afternoon, we found Miss Marie's office door opened, letting us know that she was available to speak with visitors.

"Hello, Miss Marie," I said, tapping on the door, waiting for an invitation to enter her office.

She looked up from her work and said, "What a surprise! Come on in." Her beautiful smile always made us feel welcome. Alex presented her with the shiny green plant that he was hiding behind his back.

"Oh, how beautiful, Alex. Thank you," she said, beaming as she set it on her desk. Looking around the room, we saw the little gifts of love that we had given her over the year. She had them carefully arranged on a bookshelf alongside her other cherished nick-nacks. The small glass dish of a boy and his dog was sitting on her desk filled with paper clips.

"Miss Marie, where did you get this cute little dish?" Alex asked timidly, curious to hear her response.

"Oh, that's a gift that someone very special gave me. I keep it right here in front of me. It reminds me that someone cares." By this time, Alex and I were *grinning from ear to ear.* Miss Marie's eyes twinkled, revealing that she knew we were her secret admirers. "It was you, Alex, wasn't it?"

"Yes, Miss Marie! I gave you the dog dish. It used to be mine," Alex revealed joyfully.

"Thank you, Alex. This means the world to me, knowing that you remembered me this way," she said with a big smile.

Alex looked at me, and then at Miss Marie, and said, "Well, we're not secret pals anymore—but now we're special friends." She came from behind her desk and gave us a warm embrace.

It is easy to get bogged down with routines and schedules, and become self-focused. In honoring the Lord by blessing others, we end up being the ones who are truly blessed. The end of "self" was the beginning of a precious friendship. Miss Marie is a wonderful friend and mentor to our family. We thank the Lord for blessing us with our dear friend.

"Now that you have purified yourselves by obeying the truth so that you have sincere love for your brothers, love one another deeply, from the heart." 1 Peter 1:22

Discussion

What do you do in those times of boredom or discouragement when you are tempted to think only of yourself? Is there someone special in your life who might not realize how much you value them? What can you do for them to show your gratitude? What are some ways God quietly blesses us each day that we take for granted (e.g., water, air, sunshine)?

Scripture

"Not to us, O Lord, not to us but to your name be the glory, because of your love and faithfulness." Psalm 115:1

"But when you give to the needy, do not let your left hand know what your right hand is doing." Matthew 6:3

"Each of you should look not only to your own interests, but also to the interests of others." Philippians 2:4

"Dear children, let us not love with words or tongue but with actions and in truth." 1 John 3:18

Song

"You Are My Sunshine" and "What A Friend We Have In Jesus"

Application

Make an "encouragement list" of things to do for others when you are bored or discouraged. Brainstorm with your family and think of ways that you can show your appreciation to a dear friend or mentor. Make a gift basket and fill with small, sacrificial tokens of affection for your loved one. Think of how you can give their gift to them discreetly—make it a surprise.

Idiom

Caught my eye means something that grabbed my attention.
Grinning from ear to ear means to look extremely happy.

Prayer

Thank the Lord for bringing that special person into your life. Pray a blessing over them.

Chapter 20

The Temple

"Open my eyes that I may see
wonderful things in your law."

PSALM 119:18

The activity began at the crack of dawn. We sat in our living room gazing out the window watching a crew clear the property across the street. The saws were so loud they sounded like they were in our house. The busy cranes and bulldozers carried away the sawed downed trees. Watching a tall man in the middle of the road with orange flags directing traffic, we knew that this signaled a changing look for our quiet neighborhood.

"I wonder what they're going to do with all that wood." Alex asked, wide-eyed with wonder.

"Maybe they're going to use it to build a house," I guessed. We returned to our morning devotions.

I continued reading, trying to speak over the ear-wrenching squeals of the chain saws. "So he built the temple and completed it, roofing it with beams and cedar planks" (1 Kings 6:9).

"Mother, do you think I could build something great like the temple when I grow up?"

Setting the Bible down on the table, I motioned for Alex. "Come here, and let me feel those big muscles. Yes Sir, young man, with God's help you will build great things." We continued our reading on the building of Solomon's temple.

Morning devotions were uplifting and encouraging. The story of the temple building captivated Alex. He was interested in every detail and wanted to create something of his very own. A renewed desire for the reading of God's Word was sparked in his heart and mind.

On our way home from work one day, Alex spotted a heap of wood on the side of the road near our house.

"Can we stop and ask for that wood, Mother?" he asked, pointing to the pile.

"What would you do with all that wood?"

"I would save it until I had enough to build something great," Alex said, eyeing the leftover lumber. There were bits and pieces of every shape and size. He walked to the neighbor's house and asked for the discarded wood and was granted permission to remove it from the curb. He was *busy as a beaver* for hours, piling the treasured lumber in our yard.

"Mom, I know just what I'll build with all that wood," he told me at bedtime.

"What would that be?" I asked as I turned out the lights.

"I'm going to build something special for Penny, just like Solomon built something special for God."

"That's a great idea, Alex. I can't wait to see it!"

Early the next morning, I was awakened by the sound of the squeaky dresser drawers coming from his bedroom. Alex came out of his room dressed in his overalls. His face shone with the radiant confidence of a master builder. He proceeded to the backyard where his pile of lumber waited to be constructed.

I watched from the kitchen window as Alex roamed about carefully placing his prized wood throughout the yard. After some time, there was a knock on the door. Alex was standing there with a large Rubbermaid trash can that was as big as he was.

"Mother, would you open the door, please?"

"Where did you find that trash can?" I asked with surprise. "I thought I threw it away."

"It was over there in the corner behind our house." The look on his face was that of someone who discovered buried treasure.

"Can I please have this trash can, Mom?"

"Sure, it's no use to me anymore. What will you do with it?" I asked.

"You'll see; it's a surprise!" he answered. My quick nod of approval dismissed him, and he was off to continue his backyard building adventure.

I kept busy inside, but I still had one eye on the backyard to make sure Alex was *safe and sound*. The morning air buzzed with the flurry of his busy body toting his supply of nails, hammer, and wood. It was heart-warming to watch Alex construct this work of his own design.

"How's it coming along out there?" I asked, poking my head around the corner of the back door.

"I'm almost finished. Don't come out just yet," he said with a serious look on his face.

It was not long before I heard the thud of the hammer and nails on the carport pavement. "Okay, Mom, you can come out now, but close your eyes. And bring Penny on her leash, too."

Penny waited anxiously at the backdoor, jumping and wagging her tail with excitement. "We're ready," I said as I carefully secured her collar.

Alex came to the opened door, and took me by the hand, making sure that my eyes were closed tight. Penny heeled by my side on her chain, just happy to be part of the parade to the backyard.

"Okay, open your eyes now, Mother." When I opened my eyes, I saw rows of boards laid out like a train track. There were levels and heights of every size of wood, carefully arranged. On one end was the large rubber trash can, with a hole in the bottom, big enough to crawl through. He had taken our old red picnic table benches and nailed splinters and scraps of wood to them, building a little ladder up to what looked like a runway.

"Come here, Penny." Alex said, gently leading her up the wooden steps. Guiding her down and around the wooden maze, Alex led his precious pup to and through the custom made obstacle course. Penny hesitated when she approached the narrow bottom of the rubber trash can, but was able to trust her master, Alex, to guide her safely through the course.

"Do you like it, Mom? I think Penny likes it." Alex held his shoulders up high, his smile wide.

"Yes, Son, it's brilliant. You're right, Penny likes it too! What a gallant effort to build something for good use like this. You and Penny will have lots of fun."

Alex's obstacle course was a monument of planning, hard work, and discipline. Our morning devotions planted vision and inspiration deep within Alex, and a desire to glorify God with the work of his hands. The examples we read in the Bible exemplify what our lives can look like when we set our hands to do noble and honorable things. We are most grateful to God for His Word, a cherished and valued treasure.

"Do not conform any longer to the pattern of this world, but be transformed by the renewing of your mind. Then you will be able to test and approve what God's will is— his good, pleasing and perfect will." Romans 12:2

Discussion

What is your favorite Bible story? What character qualities are illustrated in your favorite Bible story? What does it mean to "renew" your mind? What would you create or build if you could invent anything? How does reading the Bible encourage you to live your life for God's glory?

Scripture

"What you decide on will be done, and light will shine on your ways." Job 22:28

"The LORD will fulfill his purpose for me; your love, O LORD, endures forever—do not abandon the works of your hands." Psalm 138:8

"Commit to the LORD whatever you do, and your plans will succeed." Proverbs 16:3

"All Scripture is God-breathed and is useful for teaching, rebuking, correcting and training in righteousness, so that the man of God may be thoroughly equipped for every good work." 2 Timothy 3:16

Song

"The B-I-B-L-E" and "May The Mind Of Christ My Savior"

Application

Study topics of interest from the Bible (e.g., Ark of the Covenant). Memorize the books of the Bible or disciples' names. Write a script for a play of your favorite Bible story. Make costumes and props. Children love to perform for guests. Hunt for scrap building materials. Design and build a unique dwelling for your pet. Obedience training is a fun and simple skill to learn. Even the novice can teach an old dog new tricks.

Idiom

Safe and sound means securely out of harm's way.
Busy as a beaver means working very hard.

Prayer

Ask the Lord to encourage and inspire you through reading His Word.

Chapter 21

My Cup Overflows

"You anoint my head with oil; my cup overflows."

PSALM 23:5B

"Please help me load the car, and then you can start reading your book; I'll be right there." Alex gathered his backpack for the day's on-the-job homeschool training. The coffee I made over an hour ago sat untouched in the pot. What started out as a hot latte was converted to a cold frappe left over from the early morning brew.

The cup that I pulled out of the cabinet was the only coffee cup that I owned. It was pink with flowers and had a broken handle. I recently looked at a few garage sales for a replacement but never found one. This was not something I was interested in spending a lot of time doing. The broken handle was not a problem for me anyway, since the cup still fit snuggly in the car's cup holder.

"It looks like you need a new coffee cup, Mom." Alex made a similar comment every time I used that broken cup.

"I'll get one soon," I'd answer. My heart was touched when he noticed small things like that.

Later in the week, I went to use my old broken cup when it cracked in two when I poured hot coffee in it. As we walked out the door to the car, Alex suggested, "Let's pray, Mother. You need a new coffee cup."

"Great idea, Alex. Let's pray." I was humbled by his readiness to seek his Heavenly Father.

On our way to work, he prayed, "Lord, you know that my Mom's heart's desire would be to have a shiny new coffee cup. I pray that soon she will be able to buy one. Thank you, Lord."

We finished work early that day. On the way home, we passed by a department store, and I decided to stop on the *spur of the moment*. I knew we could not buy anything, but I just had the itch to look.

"Why are we stopping here?" Alex asked with an innocent curiosity.

"Oh, I just want to browse," I answered nonchalantly. We wandered through the aisles and eventually made our way to the back of the store where there was a clearance table of dishes. Stacked with the rest of the colorful glassware, there were coffee cups of every imaginable size and color.

A pretty orange mug on the table was set aside with no match in sight. *Hmm, this isn't too bad. It's on sale*, I told myself. I headed to the check-out line with the cup in hand and waited for my turn. Alex was standing close behind me.

"Mom, are you going to buy that cup?"

Leaning toward him, I whispered, "Yes, it's on sale." He watched me reach into my purse for my checkbook.

I was next in line to check out. "Mother, are you sure you're going to write a check for one coffee cup?" He whispered in a soft and caring manner. My conscience started to tug at me, reminding me that I had taught Alex to wait for the right timing when buying anything new. My budgeting priorities were being put to the test.

Ouch, I thought. *He knows me too well, I can't write a check for one cup. What am I thinking?* I returned the coffee cup to the table with the other marked down glassware.

During the ride home, we had a chance to talk about what happened in the store. Alex's perception of the incident in the store was encouraging and insightful.

"That's what happens when we just want to look, Mom, right?" he sweetly asked.

"You're right, Alex. I was tempted when I made the choice to go into the store just to look at the cups."

"I'm really proud of you, Mother, for putting the cup back. Remember when we prayed this morning that the Lord would provide you with a coffee cup at just the right time?"

"Yes, I remember. The Lord has always shown us that He will provide for our needs."

As I saw Alex express his trust in the Lord's provision, suddenly the urgent need for a cup was forgotten.

I pulled into the carport, and, as usual, Alex was the first one out of the car. He dashed to the backdoor to wait for me. "Mom, look here; it's a present," he proclaimed, pointing to a pretty gold gift bag hanging on the doorknob.

"Just a second, I'll be right there," I called.

Alex ran up to the car, waving the gift bag with a small card attached.

"Mom, who do you think it's from?" he anxiously asked.

I opened the little envelope and read the card aloud. "Dear Lynnie, I've been thinking of you and miss you. Love, Bets."

"Bets" is short for Betsy, a dear friend we had not seen for quite a while. Our busy schedules had not allowed us to stay in contact for some time.

I opened the gift bag, and I could hardly believe my eyes. Wrapped in beautiful gold tissue paper was the largest, most beautiful coffee cup I had ever seen. It was green, white, and gold with a picture of an angel holding a harp.

"Mother, can you believe it? God sent you a beautiful coffee cup!"

I stood there and cried like a little girl as I admired the detail of the painting on the cup. This special gift was given with love. I called my sweet friend Betsy and thanked her for the beautiful cup, telling her what had happened that day.

The only words she had to say were, "Lynnie, I can't explain it, but the Lord brought you to my mind today. When I saw this cup, I thought of you."

The gift was not only in the cup, but in the prayer, the trust, and the love it represented. My cup overflowed with heavenly blessings. Our faith increased, and we saw once more that we could wait on the Lord for even our smallest need.

"Every good and perfect gift is from above, coming down from the Father of the heavenly lights, who does not change like shifting shadows." James 1:17

Discussion

Can you recall a specific prayer that God answered in an unexpected way? Do you have a need you are waiting for God to fill? Will you trust and thank Him today, leaving the results in His hands? Why do you appreciate good things more when you have to wait for them? Can you recall a gift you were surprised to receive?

Scripture

"I will lift up the cup of salvation and call on the name of the LORD." Psalm 116:13

"I say to myself, 'The LORD is my portion; therefore I will wait for him.'" Lamentations 3:24

"Blessed are those who hunger and thirst for righteousness, for they will be filled." Matthew 5:6

"And my God will meet all your needs according to his glorious riches in Christ Jesus." Philippians 4:19

Song

"Bless The Lord O My Soul" and "Fill My Cup Lord (I Lift It Up Lord)"

Application

Craft a "blessing cup." Write down how the Lord provides for your every need, and keep your notes in the cup. These remembrances will be a great encouragement while you wait on the Lord for an answer to a particular prayer. Make "budget bins" out of small, plastic containers. Label them with different categories. Bless someone anonymously who you see has a special need.

Idiom

Spur of the moment means suddenly or impulsively.

Prayer

Thank the Lord for the many ways He blesses you. Ask Him to show you how you can bless someone else.

Chapter 22

His Banner Over Me Is Love

"We will shout for joy when you are victorious and will lift up our banners in the name of our God."

PSALM 20:5A

Penny sat at the back door and whined. Her droopy ears and sad, black eyes begged to go outside. It took a lot of prompting to get me out the door that chilly day, but once I set my foot on the sidewalk, I was glad I did. The first step is always the hardest.

"Come on, Alex. Let's take Penny for a walk."

"Alright, Mom. I'll grab her leash."

I went to get my jacket, and, before I knew it, they were out the door *full speed ahead*, leaving me trailing behind. They ran at least a block ahead of me, occasionally turning around to make sure I was following.

"Mother, we're waiting for you," Alex called out.

"You go on ahead," I motioned. They continued on as I worked hard to catch up with them.

"Let's walk down to the lake," Alex shouted. "I want to climb the trees."

"Okay, I'm coming," I gasped, pushing myself harder. I focused on getting to the end of the road. There was a stop sign at that point of the route which marked the downhill path toward the small lake.

"One, two, three," I puffed, holding tightly to the cold metal pole at the stop sign. "Four, five, six," I counted. This was also the landmark where I stopped to do my calf-raise exercises. Racing downhill all the way, Alex and Penny had already reached the lake. I finished my exercises on the corner and began my own descent toward the lake.

The quaint lake was a beautiful, quiet place surrounded by big oak trees. Here and there, tall, spiky pine trees rose majestically. The water surface was still, and the scent of pine was wafting through the chilly air. I was glad that I had come for a walk.

"Mom, would you take Penny so I can climb the trees?" Alex panted.

"Sure, give her to me. Have fun and be careful."

Alex ran off like a squirrel, jumping onto the closest limb he could reach.

"Look, Mom," he hollered, as he dangled from an overhanging branch.

"Watch out, hold tight," I said and then prayed as any mother would do.

Penny tugged and pulled as we walked around the lake. I made sure her leash was wrapped tightly around my hand. The last thing I wanted was to wash a cold, wet dog when I got home. I was keeping an eye on Alex up in the tree, watching to make sure he did not fall. Following Penny's energetic lead, I assured her that she was not forgotten.

"Alex, not too high," I insisted as I gazed up into the trees.

"Don't worry, Mom. I'll be careful," he said, looking my way.

Suddenly, out of nowhere I heard, "Quack, quack," and my casual stroll turned into a fierce tug-of-war. A big mallard duck went skimming over the lake. Penny darted toward the water, dragging me behind her. Before I had a chance to stop her, she sprinted powerfully toward the duck, aiming to get her paws on the mallard that was flying to the opposite side of the lake.

"Mother, be careful," Alex called out from the tree.

"Penny! Come, Girl. No!" I cried. Before I knew it, we were slipping down the muddy slope.

She quickly pulled me down the embankment to the water's edge. I was trying to hold her back, knowing we were just seconds from landing in the water. Penny was barking out of control, drooling at the sight of the feathered target that was now calmly resting on the farthest bank.

"Down, Girl. No!" I pleaded, pulling and tugging right back.

"Mom, hold on!" I heard Alex shout from behind. Glancing over my shoulder, I saw him jumping from the limb, waving his sweatshirt over his head. "Penny! Here, Girl. Come here!" Alex cried. "Come, Penny, come!" he commanded, charging toward me, still waving his sweatshirt over his head like a banner on a battlefield.

With each step that Alex advanced, Penny pulled another step further in the opposite direction until I could no longer hold her back. I slipped to the ground, landing flat on my backside. "Mother, hold on, I'm coming!" Alex shouted.

Penny pulled me all the way into the lake's shallow water. She was barking and splashing, trying to swim to the other side of the lake. I held on with all my might so that she did not get away. When Alex arrived at my side, his flailing sweatshirt managed to get Penny's attention and focus back our way.

"Calm down now, Girl," Alex persisted, settling his wet pup.

"Oh hurry, help me up," I cried as Alex reached to retrieve me out of the chilling water. He pried away the leash that was tightly wrapped around my hand. Penny knew she had misbehaved and hung her head in shame. She knew she was *in the doghouse.*

Once on my feet, I stood there shivering while Alex took his sweatshirt and wrapped it tightly around my shoulders. "Are you okay, Mother?" he asked as he gently picked out the many pine needles that were stuck to my clothes.

"Yes, Son, just a little wet and cold. Thank you, Alex," I said with a hug. "You saved the day!" Our journey home felt much longer than usual. Penny heeled right by Alex's side all the way home.

We spent that evening wrapped in our warm blankets enjoying hot cocoa, reminiscing over the day's events. Penny slept close by, curled up in her bed. It was a picture-perfect end to a banner day.

"It all happened so fast," I told Alex. "I looked up, and all I saw was your sweatshirt that looked like a banner waving over your head. One minute I was watching you in the tree, and the next minute you were rescuing me from a runaway hound," I said with a smile. "I didn't even have to call—you were there in an instant."

"That's how God protects us!" Alex declared. "His banner of love is always over us. He knows exactly what we need before we even ask."

Mallards are most often found in small, tranquil lakes. The Mallard duck is able to take flight straight up from the water thirty-six feet to clear tree tops. Mallards fly at a speed of forty to fifty miles per hour. The male Mallard is called a drake and is the most beautiful of the Mallards with a bright yellow bill and green head. The female Mallard is blotchy, drab, and brown in color.

Discussion

Do you know where the first banner appears in the Bible (Genesis 9:12–13, when God sent a rainbow)? What did Christ dying on the cross proclaim to the entire world? How can we declare our love for God by the way we live? How does God demonstrate His banner of protection over you? How can you practice your chivalry at home?

Scripture

"For the eyes of the LORD range throughout the earth to strengthen those whose hearts are fully committed to him." 2 Chronicles 16:9a

"The righteous cry out, and the LORD hears them; he delivers them from all their troubles." Psalm 34:17

"Since my youth, O God, you have taught me, and to this day I declare your marvelous deeds." Psalm 71:17

"He lifts up a banner for the distant nations, he whistles for those at the ends of the earth. Here they come, swiftly and speedily!" Isaiah 5:26

Song

"His Banner Over Me Is Love" and "Hosannah" and "Onward Christian Soldiers"

Application

In the Bible, banners are used for identification, declaration, and worship. Craft a banner or flag declaring the goodness and faithfulness of the Lord. Write scriptures or attributes of God on them. Use them for display and worship. Use an atlas to match countries and their flags. Visit your favorite pond and feed the ducks. Play Duck, Duck, Goose.

Idiom

Full speed ahead means with all speed and strength.
In the doghouse means facing correction for misbehaving.

Prayer

Declare gratitude to the Lord for His banner of love over you.

Chapter 23

Hoop Dreams

"Perseverance must finish its work so that you may be mature and complete, not lacking anything."

JAMES 1:4

By all appearances, this was a typical school day. However, there were greater lessons to be learned than were planned. Sitting at my desk in the schoolroom and looking directly out the window in front of my eyes stood the tall basketball hoop. It was calling my name to come out and play.

Trying to ignore the overwhelming distraction, I put my nose and eyes back into my book and tried to stay focused on my math studies. But as the time passed, instead of subtracting the numbers in my math lesson, I found myself counting down the minutes until I would be finished and able to go play basketball.

I looked out the other window of my school room across the field, and I saw one of my favorite birds, the American kestrel, perched high above the ground on a power line. While I sat in my chair squirming around, I noticed the bird's gaze fixed directly in front of him. He sat there motionlessly attentive, watching for the slightest movement for what potentially could be his lunch.

I was instantly brought back to reality by the footsteps of my Mother coming down the hallway. I must have been daydreaming for a while—well, actually, quite a long time. As she entered the room, I tried with great effort to turn my attention back to my studies.

"How are you doing, Alex? Do you need anything?"

I knew in my heart that I had the responsibility to do the work that was right in front of me, yet I struggled to keep putting the pencil to the paper. "What can I do to help you? Are you at a standstill?" she asked.

What was keeping me from completing my schoolwork? I asked myself. Was it the view of the basketball hoop outside that was distracting me, or was it my own lack of self-discipline?

"I'm struggling to keep focused," I confessed. In any case, I was in need of help. I turned around in my chair, and my Mother was standing there with a big smile on her face.

"Alex, with God's help, I know you can do it," she assured me. She quoted Philippians 4:13 to encourage me, "Remember, 'I can do everything through him who gives me strength.'"

"Alex, do you want to come with me to the store? We can go for a little ride and get some fresh air." I gladly put down my pencil. This was the perfect time to take a break. We passed the basketball hoop as we exited our driveway.

"That rim has been beckoning me all morning," I said with longing. "It's been tough resisting the temptation to go out and play." The imaginary *ants in my pants* seemed to wiggle out to my arms and legs. All I wanted to do was go outside and shoot a few hoops and dribble the basketball for a while.

When we drove under the power line, we noticed the beautiful kestrel, still on his perch. *Wow, he hadn't moved an inch!* I thought. As we continued, my Mom explained with an understanding tone in her voice, "It's important that we persevere in all we do, Alex. Remember Noah? He persevered for many years, building the ark one board at a time. I imagine Noah must have gotten distracted from time to time."

"Yes, he probably faced many distractions, too," I answered.

"Noah's diligence and obedience produced a hope for mankind of God's love and faithfulness to His people," Mom went on to say. We talked about how we have to stay on task with the work that the Lord gives us each day. My Mother knows how to encourage me.

"Look, Mom, the kestrel is still sitting there," I commented on our way back from the store. He was perched in front of me in plain view. Then suddenly, *out of the clear blue sky*, he sprang from the line and dove down into the open field.

"Where did he go?" I squinted, looking for him among the tall grass.

Just as quickly as he dove to the ground, he shot back up. "Look Mother, there he goes; he's got something in his talons!" He swiftly landed back on his perch, clenching his afternoon catch of the day. "Maybe it's a lizard or a little snake."

In that moment, it all came together for me. I remembered that the kestrel had been sitting on that old power line all morning long and had not moved, not even once. I thought about how much patience and attentiveness he showed, keeping his focus on the goal of catching his prey. I saw that perseverance means focus with a purpose, and that patience is a requirement to reach goals. Then I asked myself, *What could I achieve if I practiced the same habits of the kestrel?*

As soon as we got home, I ran into my schoolroom and turned my desk around so I would not be facing the window or the view of the basketball hoop. I sat down at my desk, bowed my head, and prayed, "Dear Lord, please help me stay focused on my school work. Thank you for the beautiful example of the kestrel, and how he demonstrated to me how to persevere. Please help me focus for the rest of the day. Amen."

The afternoon felt long as I struggled to finish the rest of my studies. When I was tempted to think about things other than the lesson before me, I paused and remembered what I had seen earlier that morning when the kestrel was rewarded for his perseverance and focus.

I am grateful for the unique way that God taught me this lesson through His creation. I am also thankful to the Lord for my Mother who is patient with me and encourages me to continue in the things that God has placed before me.

The American kestrel can be easily identified by two black stripes on its white face. This bird of prey has very keen eyesight and eight sharp talons which help it hunt prey. The kestrel eats insects, reptiles, and small mammals. The American kestrel is the smallest falcon in North America measuring nine to twelve inches in length.

Discussion

How did the American kestrel demonstrate perseverance? What can you do to get back on track when you get restless during your schoolwork? What is an example of a time when you persevered through a trial? What were the fruits of your perseverance? Why is obedience necessary in order to persevere?

Scripture

"And Noah did all the Lord commanded him." Genesis 7:5

"But ask the animals, and they will teach you, or the birds of the air, and they will tell you;" Job 12:7

"No temptation has seized you except what is common to man. And God is faithful; he will not let you be tempted beyond what you can bear. But when you are tempted, he will also provide a way out so that you can stand up under it." 1 Corinthians 10:13

Song

"Be Thou My Vision" and "The Joy Of The Lord Is My Strength"

Application

Set small, daily goals and write them down. Record how perseverance assisted you in moving forward to grander objectives. Research your favorite animal. Discover what valuable character lessons you can learn from its habits. Make a placemat by drawing a picture of your favorite animal. Laminate your placemat to make it last a long time. Rearrange and spruce up your study space to help you focus better.

Idiom

Out of the clear blue sky means totally unexpected.
Ants in my pants means excessive restlessness.

Prayer

Ask your Heavenly Father to help you persevere with your schoolwork and other work He has set before you.

Chapter 24

Bench Press

"Be still, and know that I am God; I will be exalted
among the nations, I will be exalted in the earth."

PSALM 46:10

Summertime marked the height of activity at the retreat center. A large group was coming on Friday for an action-packed weekend of Vacation Bible School. Our job this week was to finish painting the aged but sturdy benches that would seat the over one-hundred scheduled guests. It was already Tuesday afternoon, which left us only two and a half days to complete our work.

We had not made it up the hill yet to work on the benches, because we had been building a rock fence around the bottom of our house. The frequent visits of a skunk digging under our house had been a major distraction over the past few months. My top priority now was to discourage any further visits from our smelly acquaintance.

On this particular afternoon, I drove our van up the hill to the outdoor chapel where the Vacation Bible School would be held. The last two benches we needed to paint sat outside the chapel. Alex and I pulled the benches out onto the grass near the pavilion. It seemed like it was going to be a pretty easy job to finish.

"I can get started on this by myself, Alex. Why don't you go back home and work on your schoolwork. You can help me when you're finished."

"Alright, Mom. I'll see you in a couple of hours."

These two benches had to be scraped and sanded by hand. I did not have a lot of experience painting, so I had not considered how long the prep work would take. Using a steel wool brush that had a metal edge, I worked to scrape off the chipped paint. Any splintered wood that could snag the children's clothes had to be sanded. Splinters are not fun. I imagined all the children sitting on the freshly painted benches, listening to the teacher talk about Jesus.

As I hurried to finish, my mind wandered to the rock fence that still needed to be done. I stopped my sanding. That would just have to do. My eyes had sawdust in them, and my hands were sore and tired from all the scraping. I could see Alex coming up the hill. Help was on the way.

"How's it coming along, Mom? How much work is left?"

"Hi, Alex. You're a welcomed sight," I said with a sigh. "I'm finished sanding, and the benches are ready to paint."

Alex liked to paint, so I trusted he would know if the wood was ready. Running his hand across a bench, he commented, "There are still some rough spots. Let's sand them out."

I felt pressed for time, thinking about the rock fence and how we should get home to work on it. We quickly sanded the benches a little more, and eventually the wood was smooth enough to take a coat of paint. Alex applied the chocolate-brown paint with ease, not missing a stroke. I thought to myself, *It will be dark soon. I can almost see that skunk trying to dig under the house right now.* I cringed.

"Alex, I think that looks just fine. We'd better get going."

He could see that I was really pressing hard to finish the bench project, trying to get on to my own "pressing issue." We left the benches outside to dry overnight before adding a second coat. I rushed to gather all the brushes, rags, and the five-gallon bucket of paint.

"Mom, I'll take the things to the shed."

"Thank you, Alex, but I'd prefer you head back home and start filling in the rocks around the house. It will be dark soon, and we're getting *down to the wire.*"

"Sure, Mom, I'll see you later at the house."

I put the paint and utensils in the back of my van. Leaving the pavilion, I circled to go back down the hill. As I made the turn, I heard a loud thud. *Oh no! It couldn't be. It just couldn't happen! It must be something else*, I thought.

Stunned, I put the van in park, jumped out, ran to the back, and threw open the hatch. There, spilled over in the back of our beautiful gray van, was the five gallons of chocolate-brown paint. It ran all the way down the floor boards to the front seats. The paint was two inches deep. My mind raced when I realized that daylight was running out, and my vision to complete the fence was rapidly fading. I called Alex on my cell phone and asked him to come back quickly.

I rolled up my sleeves and began scooping out the paint onto the grass. My shoes were quickly filling up with the dripping brown paint as the carpet was absorbing as much as it could hold. Alex came rushing up the hill and found me covered in brown from my chin to the soles of my feet. I started to cry, "Just look at this mess!"

"Mother, what happened?" He asked rushing to my aid.

"When I tried to turn the car, the tub of paint spilled over. I didn't double-check to see if the lid was on tight. I was too busy fretting about finishing the fence." We headed back to the house and began the long, laborious task of removing the paint from the van.

And what a mess it was. We both tried to scoop the paint, and now soap and water, out of the back of the van. I sat down for a moment on the back porch to gather my composure. I called my friend sobbing and told her about what had just happened. Her first words were, "Is this another skunk tale?"

I had to confess to her that my fear of a skunk returning to our house set into motion the day's chain of events that ended with my van full of chocolate-brown paint. She scolded me for worrying and reminded me that it did not help a thing. The idea that we would possibly be spending another night with the rock fence unfinished troubled me. Our house might once again be the target of a stinky, nighttime prowler.

We feverishly attempted to remove as much paint from the van as we could. The pressing paint project did not get finished because we had to order new paint which would not arrive by Friday. The camp would be short two benches for the Vacation Bible School. I could see that I let my thoughts about a smelly skunk rule my mind that day.

As we stood watching the remaining paint and water drip from the van, Alex comforted me, "You know what, Mother? Don't worry about the van, the benches, or even the rock fence. And don't worry if another smelly skunk comes around the house. Those aren't the most important things. We have each other, and we have the Lord. *Those* are the most important things." Alex prayed and thanked the Lord for these important things, and I asked the Lord to forgive me for worrying.

Skunks den under houses, vacant dwellings, caves and wood piles. Skunks are extremely curious. Male skunks den alone, but females den with other females and their young. Skunks do not hibernate like bears do, but they are dormant for the coldest period of winter.

Discussion

What prevented the benches from getting painted? How could the paint accident have been avoided? How did fretting contribute to this calamity? What is the opposite of fretting (faith and prudence)? How does God's Word instruct us to deal with an anxious spirit? What does the Bible say is important to God?

Scripture

"Therefore do not worry about tomorrow, for tomorrow will worry about itself. Each day has enough trouble of its own." Matthew 6:34

"Do not be anxious about anything, but in everything, by prayer and petition, with thanksgiving, present your requests to God. And the peace of God, which transcends all understanding, will guard your hearts and your minds in Christ Jesus. Finally, brothers, whatever is true, whatever is noble, whatever is right, whatever is pure, whatever is lovely, whatever is admirable—if anything is excellent or praiseworthy—think about such things." Philippians 4:6–8

Song

"Count Your Blessings" and "Seek Ye First"

Application

Volunteer for a work day at your church and help someone who needs assistance with house projects or yard work. Perform an extra chore around the house without being asked (e.g., clean out the family car). Knowing God's Word can cure an anxious mind. Have a "sword drill" with your family. Everyone starts with their Bibles closed. One person calls out a reference and says, "Go!" The first person to find the verse wins.

Idiom

Down to the wire means running out of time.

Prayer

Thank the Lord for at least three things for which you are grateful.

Chapter 25

Digger

"The wisdom of the prudent is to give thought to their ways, but the folly of fools is deception."

PROVERBS 14:8

The heat of the Texas summer encouraged us to delay our chores until the sun sank low behind the hills. One evening right at dusk, Alex and I went to clean the cabins in preparation for the next group that was scheduled to come. The evenings were typically quiet and uneventful, but this was not the case tonight.

Ahead of us in the distance, we saw a critter cross the road. Even though we were downwind from it, we caught a whiff of its horrible scent. "It's a skunk!" Alex shrieked.

"Well, you just *took the words right out of my mouth*," I replied. We watched him hobble—that is the way skunks walk—they do not really walk, they hobble. Hobbling and wobbling back and forth, the skunk disappeared into the trees.

"Can we follow him, Mom? I'm curious to see a skunk up close," Alex said. We dashed up the hill for a quick look.

We hid behind the dining hall near the cabins, hoping to get a closer look at the skunk. Minutes passed and we did not see him, so we waited. We tried to remain still, waiting for any kind of movement from the roaming creature, but the scent was strong. At last, when I put my nose up in the air to take a deep breath, he reappeared.

"There he goes under the picnic table," said Alex as the skunk crossed the grass and disappeared again. "Maybe he has a den under the table," he whispered. "Come on, Mom. Let's go hide behind that tree." We made a run for the tree closest to where the skunk had fled.

I thought about all the work we had to do that night and questioned my decision for this hunt. There was no sign of the skunk for the next few minutes, but the putrid smell in the air was stagnant, hovering over us like a cloud. My nose was itching, and my eyes were watering.

"Maybe he's taking a *cat nap*," Alex suggested.

"Look, there goes the little rascal!" I cried. He darted from under the picnic table to the back of an old shed. We could no longer see him from behind the tree where we were hiding. With just one small gust of wind our way, we got another good dose of skunk perfume right between the eyes. I turned my head away and squeezed my eyes shut, holding my breath with one big gasp.

Not only was Alex younger than I, he was braver and quicker, too. He made a dash for the picnic table. "Shhh," he cautioned, and the whisper carried over in my direction on the tail end of the pungent scent.

Alex signaled for me to join him. We huddled underneath the picnic table, closely following the skunk's trail. "There he is, over by the shed." Alex seemed to have night vision. On the side of the shed we could could see a small opening.

By this time it was dark. The only light was the moon that reflected the broad, white stripe that ran down the skunk's furry body. He tottered about poking his nose in the ground, looking for a place to dig. He started burrowing under the side of the shed. After a while, we could see that he was no longer digging. "He must be getting tired," said Alex. The fluffy tail on his pudgy little body lay motionless in the cool, dark earth.

Assuming that the skunk was just taking a rest, we stayed under the table to catch our breath. "What do you think he's doing now?" Alex whispered. We did not want to agitate him and provoke him to raise his tail and use his powerful weapon. "I can't see him very well," said Alex. "I think we need more light."

We quickly backtracked down the hill to our house to get a flashlight and then hurried back to the tree where we had first been hiding. Alex pointed the flashlight toward the side of the shed. We were disappointed to discover a lifeless little black and white body. The skunk was lying there with his body wedged up under the shed. He looked as still as a log. Looking closer with curiosity and fascination, we could clearly see that he was stuck.

"Alex, how could he have gotten caught under the shed like that?" I asked.

"I'm not exactly sure, Mother, but it looks like he was snooping. He was probably searching for food. He was digging in the wrong place at the wrong time and got caught."

Suddenly, his tail moved. He was alive! We kept our distance, watching him furiously work his way out of his dilemma. Wiggle and dig, wiggle and dig, at last he dug himself out of his mess. We held our noses and our breaths as "Digger the Skunk" hobbled off over the hill, his white stripe shining like a victory banner in the moonlight.

"Skunks may leave, Mom, but they're not easily forgotten," Alex noted, as he grabbed a shovel from the shed and filled in the hole that Digger had made, not wanting another skunk to follow his example.

Because of our skunk hunt, we finished our chores much later than usual. Our curiosity had gotten the best of us. We walked back home and hung our smelly clothes out on the clothes line.

"Whew! Curiosity costs," Alex confessed, "and that little skunk paid a price, too, almost the ultimate price—his life!"

"Alex, let's remember to consider the cost before we follow our noses. I'm glad we took the time to learn this lesson from a skunk."

Skunks are good diggers and forage from early evening until morning. Skunks have partially webbed toes and long, dull claws. They help them tear apart foliage and trees for food and dig dens for shelter. Skunks do not store food but will raid food from other animals. Skunks are the primary predator of the honey bee; skunks' thick fur protects them from stings.

Discussion

What does the phrase "curiosity costs" mean? Was it wise to fill in the hole at the shed? Explain why. Is there something that you are curious to learn about? Which Bible characters would you like to interview? What would you ask them? Discuss when it is, or is not, appropriate to be inquisitive.

Scripture

"The days of the blameless are known to the LORD, and their inheritance will endure forever." Psalm 37:18

"I love those who love me, and those who seek me find me." Proverbs 8:17

"Be very careful, then, how you live—not as unwise but as wise." Ephesians 5:15

Song

"Be Careful Little Eyes" and "Love Lifted Me"

Activity

Play Hide and Seek in the dark with flashlights. First, decide what unsafe places will be off-limits. Send little ones out in pairs.

Application

Make a list of at least three varied subjects that you are curious to study more (e.g., bird-watching, a new language, research family tree). Dig up weeds in the yard and garden and plant new shrubs. Re-pot small plants or flowers for your porch or window sills. Dig into the Proverbs and find out what God tells us about curiosity and prudence.

Idiom

Take the words right out of my mouth means to say what another person is thinking.
Cat nap means a short, rejuvinating rest.

Prayer

Ask the Lord to help you be curious about His Word and His ways.

Chapter 26

Flash!

*"The plans of the diligent lead to profit
as surely as haste leads to poverty."*

PROVERBS 21:5

We brought the last big garbage cans full of leaves and dumped them in the burn pile. Gladly loading the remaining empty garbage cans, we put them in the back of the golf cart.

"This is number thirteen, Mom. Do you think we can win the contest?"

"We'll do the best we can, Son." With drops of sweat running down his neck, Alex raked up the dry, crispy summer leaves with all his gusto and might. We were competing with the other residents at the camp to see who could rake up the most leaves on the grounds.

"Let's go for it, Mom. Let's rake 'til we break—break the record, that is." Alex cheered.

It was a bumpy ride to the shed where we stored the empty cans. We hit a big rock, and the hefty plastic containers rolled out one by one onto the ground. As Alex jumped out of the cart to retrieve them, he noticed a flash out of the corner of his eye. "Look, Mom, over there! Did you see that?" he asked, pointing to a grassy area. I was still looking at the rolling trash cans, but he directed my eyes to the shrubs straight ahead.

"What was it?" I asked, not seeing a thing.

"I think it was the little fox I've seen around here. It looks like he dropped something out of his mouth."

"Hurry, get in the cart," I said. "Let's go take a look."

We drove the cart over to the edge of the meadow where Alex had seen the fox dart into the bushy grass. He jumped out and ran to the sight. "Look, here's some trash he dropped; he must have been hunting for food." He pointed to the small paw prints in the dirt which he believed belonged to the scampering scavenger.

"What exactly did he look like?" I asked him.

"He was small and grayish or silver looking. I didn't get a good look. He ran through here quick as a flash!" Alex's eyes were keener than mine.

"I hope I get another look at him sometime, but he's so swift," Alex said, all *geared up* with excitement.

"Maybe next time you'll get another look at him, but let's get back to the house now and start school," I said.

Wading through the stacks of papers and books in the school room, I was able to get my hands on the small box of math flash cards. "Here you go Alex. Practice these cards, and I'll be back in ten minutes to drill you on them." I went into the kitchen to work on some meal preparation for the day. Five minutes later, Alex showed up in the kitchen.

"Mom, I'm finished."

"Already?" I answered, surprised. "That sure was fast." I silently questioned the timing. *He must already know them all,* I supposed.

"Good job, Alex. I'm going to nick-name you Flash, like the fox, because you finished so quickly." We drilled through the flash cards making two stacks. Success was not how many he got right or wrong, but rather the improvement he was making. Progress was the goal, not a perfect score. Looking at the stacks of cards I said, "Alex, let's try this again. You have more wrong than right this time. Take your time. I know you can do it."

I returned to my work in the kitchen. It seemed like only seconds when I heard him eagerly say, "This time, Mom, I'm really finished."

"Did you get through all the way to twelve?" I asked. We went through the drill one more time. Alex was sitting on the edge of his seat, trying to keep his hands folded and in front. He wanted to get through this drill in a hurry.

"You've improved a lot, Alex, but I think you can do better if you paced yourself. What do you think would happen if you spent the entire ten minutes focused on the flash cards?" He went back to study the flash cards once more, this time for the full ten minutes. The next time he completed the stack of times-tables with a score of 100%.

"Congratulations! That-a-boy, I knew you could do it," I cheered. This time his face radiated confidence. It was a joy to see that he was pleased with his success.

The gray fox we saw that morning came to my mind as we were talking. "Alex, sometimes it's okay to work quickly, but there are times when haste works against us. We're all in a hurry to finish raking up the leaves, because we want the prize," I explained. "However, when we carelessly hurry for no reason, we can end up lagging behind or, even worse, with nothing. Consider that little fox we saw this morning and how he dropped his food. Remember, your scores soared when you were diligent!"

"Mother, I realize that I rushed through my schoolwork today so that I could go out and play basketball," he confessed. "From now on, I'm going to take my time. I don't want to drop my math scores like the fox dropped his meal."

"Good thinking, Alex. Remember, *haste makes waste!*"

We steadily raked more leaves every day and won the raking contest that summer with a record-breaking thirty-eight barrels. The Bible says that diligence leads to gain, and that haste leads to want.

Foxes are omnivorous. This small, nocturnal mammal is from the dog family. A fox's hearing is so sharp they can hear a watch ticking from forty yards away. Foxes have large ears and a long, bushy tail that makes up for one-third of his body length. Foxes can run at speeds up to thirty miles per hour.

Discussion

When is it appropriate to work quickly? When is it appropriate to be steady? How can you be more diligent with your schoolwork? How can diligence help set a pattern for your daily Bible reading? How does diligence give glory to God? How does God demonstrate diligence with us?

Scripture

"I will hasten and not delay to obey your commands." Psalm 119:60

"It is not good to have zeal without knowledge, nor to be hasty and miss the way." Proverbs 19:2

"My dear brothers, take note of this: Everyone should be quick to listen, slow to speak and slow to become angry." James 1:19

Song

"Bringing In The Sheaves" and "The Steadfast Love Of The Lord"

Activity

Egg and Spoon Race. One raw egg and spoon per person. Flash to a marked line in the yard. The first one to cross the line without breaking his egg is the winner. This is definitely an outdoor game.

Application

Design flash cards to study during your spare time. Craft a poster of your own original rhyme to recite. For example, "The little gray fox made a dash in a flash, and his treat was a waste when he fled in a haste!" Have a leaf raking contest. Set a timer and see who can rake their pile the highest. Applaud any small efforts of diligence in your children.

Idiom

Geared up means prepared for upcoming action.
Haste makes waste means that when we take action too quickly, we are more likely to make errors.

Prayer

Ask the Lord to teach you how to pace yourself in your daily activities.

Chapter 27

The Pile Up

*"We demolish arguments and every
pretension that sets itself up against the
knowledge of God, and we take captive every
thought to make it obedient to Christ."*

2 CORINTHIANS 10:5

The wooded area around our house was the ideal habitat for skunks. Once again, I was awakened in the early hours by a strong scent. Armed with a can of hot pepper spray, I went to the back porch and called out, "Get away—I have skunk spray!" just in case I saw something black, white, and furry.

The hardware store around the corner offered great ideas on how to deal with skunks. By now I thought we would have run them off for good, but that had not been the case. We had spent months dealing with the pesky animals.

We were leaving the next day on a trip to Florida. We planned to visit our former church, and share about our recent mission adventure. Suitcases lay open on our living room floor. We still had quite a bit to do before we left, and I was feeling a bit overwhelmed. By early afternoon, I still had not conquered my "to-do" list. In the corner by the kitchen, a huge pile of clothes waited to be washed.

"Alex, do you have all your things together ready to pack?"

"No Ma'am, I need a lot of clothes washed. Should I do them now?"

"No, let's think about that later. We still have to go up the hill and clean the cabins." It was a holiday weekend, and the work at the camp had to be done before we left town no matter what.

"What about the rock fence, Alex? There's three more feet of rock to pile. I don't want to come back to find a skunk family living under the house." He had been building a rock barrier for some time to keep out any smelly intruders.

"Yes, Mother, I remember. And let's not forget, we have to finish the display board for the church. We can't get on that plane without it!"

"We'll just have to *play it by ear*, Alex. Let's get our work done on the hill first and then work on the fence."

I had tried hard to have everything done before now—the packing, the washing, and the chores at the camp. Unfortunately, my lack of proper planning was catching up with me. The fence was the most important thing on my mind at the time.

I only wish we would have finished the rock fence last week, I said to myself. If the rock fence was done, we would have had plenty of time to finish the other projects. I imagined what might happen if the house was not protected from the skunks. Last minute details were beginning to pile up all around us. The sun was quickly setting by the time we finished cleaning the cabins.

"Mom, I'm going down to the shed to get the pickaxe. I know you'll rest better tonight once that fence is finished."

"Thank you Alex. You're right. That will surely put my mind at ease."

I went back to the house to finish getting ready for the trip. Minutes later, I saw Alex walking up the yard carrying the pickaxe over his shoulder, prepared to complete the rock fence once and for all. THUMP, THUMP, THUMP. Alex was making progress in no time.

I was busy in the house rounding up any dirty clothes that had not made it to the wash pile. The rhythmic sound of the pickaxe was soothing to my ears. *Maybe we'll get everything done by the time we leave after all,* I hoped.

THUMP! Silence. No more thumps of the pickaxe. "Mother, come here, hurry!" I quickly ran out the door and found Alex standing in a stream of water. Water was shooting up into the air from a pipe he had punctured while digging.

"Oh no! What happened?" I cried.

"I didn't know there was a water pipe under the ground. Quick, call someone!"

I ran into the house and called the camp office. The recording said, "The office will be closed for the weekend." *Now what do we do?* I asked myself. *We have a plane to catch in less than twelve hours.* Through the window, I saw Alex trying to stand on the broken pipe, attempting to plug up the hole. The fountain of water spewed everywhere. He was soaked from head to toe.

The neighbor that lived across the street heard Alex and came running over, hollering, "Hold tight, I'm coming. What happened?" Mr. Newburn quickly surveyed the situation. After taking a look at the broken pipe, he dashed over to his truck and came back carrying a big wrench.

"We'll have to turn off all the water in the house. I can't get the part I need to fix it until Monday morning," he said.

Oh, no, I thought. *We won't have any water for the house. How will I wash the dirty clothes? I still have the mission presentation to prepare. How will we shower? It's dark. What about the rock fence? How will we ever make it on the plane in less than twelve hours?*

I threw up my hands and asked, "What are we going to do now?"

"You're welcome to use the water at our house if you'd like," Mr. Newburn offered.

As Mr. Newburn helped us turn off our water and gather our laundry, my worries slowly turned into gratefulness. It could have been a lot worse. What would have happened if the neighbors were not home? But they were, and we were able to wash our clothes at their house and finish the preparations for our trip. The mission report was completed, and Alex and Mr. Newburn finished building the rock fence with the help of flashlights. We got to bed much later than we had planned, but we rested well.

As I fell asleep that night, I reflected on the kindness of our neighbor. I left the skunks in the woods where they belonged and the water pipe in Mr. Newburn's care. My perspective was restored as I pondered the faithfulness of the Lord. This experience taught me to take special care over my thoughts and priorities.

We thankfully made it to the airport on time. We were excited to tell everyone about the faithfulness of the Lord in both this experience and during our travels on our mission trip.

Hot pepper spray is an effective skunk deterrent. Skunks spray when they feel threatened or frightened. Skunks stomp their feet and raise their tails when alarmed, but they stand still to spray. A skunk can spray a predator from as far as ten feet away. Skunks can spray several times in succession.

Discussion

How could this pile-up have been prevented? How can you "take captive" your thoughts? What is one big thing that distracts you from accomplishing your goals? How can you overcome this distraction? What Bible stories illustrate the importance of proper planning?

Scripture

"He lifted me out of the slimy pit, out of the mud and mire; he set my feet on a rock and gave me a firm place to stand." Psalm 40:2

"Many are the plans in a man's heart, but it is the LORD's purpose that prevails." Proverbs 19:21

"He answered: 'Love the Lord your God with all your heart and with all your soul and with all your strength and with all your mind'; and, 'Love your neighbor as yourself.'" Luke 10:27

Song

"I Surrender All" and "Deep and Wide"

Activity

Plan a "Mission Water Project." Research how much water one person uses in a day. (It takes ten gallons for one load of laundry.) Purchase one large bottle of drinking water to serve with a "missions" meal. Discuss your research. Use the plastic water bottle as a bank. Create ways for your children to earn extra money for the water project. Donate the funds to a missionary or a specific ministry that provides water to the needy.

Application

Set a timer for three minutes to reflect and ponder; make a list of future goals according to priority and discuss what you have written. Play a game of Pick-Up Sticks. Draw this poster and place it where your family will be most inspired: Prior Proper Planning Prevents Problems.

Idiom

Play it by ear means to make plans along the way and not ahead of time.

Prayer

Ask the Lord to teach you to keep your priorities in their proper place.

Chapter 28

Dripping

"Bear with each other and forgive whatever grievances you may have against one another. Forgive as the Lord forgave you."

COLOSSIANS 3:13

Alex stretched high on his toes, reaching up into the big oak tree with a rake. Down came the sticky gray web that was hanging from the branches, entangled in the rake. Tiny green worms wriggled in the web. They dangled through the smoky mesh like merry lights on a Christmas tree. These pesky insects, called canker worms, appeared during the spring months in Texas.

After sweeping a path to the doorway, Alex came into the house and found that he had several of the small, fluorescent crawlers on his shirt and in his hair. He stood in front of the bathroom mirror, carefully pulling them off one by one. Swiping my hand across the back of his shirt, a brown stain appeared.

"Look at this," I said, holding the small, curled-up worm.

"These worms leave stains. Give me your shirt, and let me try to wash it out." I went straight to the laundry room where I sprayed and scrubbed, rubbed and dubbed, trying to remove the brown ooze. After a valiant effort, I tossed his shirt in the washer and hoped for the best.

Today we were going sight-seeing with a group of Korean high school students who were visiting the camp. Walking out to the car, I reminded Alex, "Watch out overhead for the dangling worms; they'll stain your clothes. I called the exterminator, and he'll be here tomorrow to spray the trees."

"I hope that will take care of those messy pests," Alex remarked.

We went to visit the natural caverns down the road from our house. Ten of us packed tightly into our van like a can of sardines. As I looked in my rear view mirror, I saw several of the young men talking in a low voice.

"Hey, guys, why don't you share with us?" I wondered if they were saying something we would all be interested to hear.

"Oh, it's nothing," I heard someone say, but I could not make out who it was. When we arrived at the cavern park, the car erupted with excitement and expectancy.

"Here we are! We made it, let's go!" they all cheered, as we piled out of the van.

We wandered through the dark, humid passageways admiring the beauty of the caverns. Moisture trickled to the ground making shallow puddles impossible to avoid. We were dripping from the humidity as we exited the caves seeking something to satisfy our hunger and thirst. To our delight, we discovered a gift shop that offered refreshing and satisfying ice cream cones. We sat outside under the shade trees enjoying the cold, tasty treats. Several of the young men gathered to one side in a group.

"Alex, is everything going alright with the guys?" I asked.

"I'm not sure, Mom. I think they might be talking about someone."

"I'm sorry to hear that, Alex. Words can really hurt."

His countenance reminded me that he had experienced this before. "Yes, Mom, I remember. Unkind words do hurt."

Kido, one of the young Korean boys, sat across the table by himself. "Come over here and sit with us," I invited. "You seem so somber. *A penny for your thoughts.*"

He quietly joined us.

"Are you enjoying the summer so far, Kido?"

"Yes, Ma'am. I sure love Texas, and I sure love this ice cream cone," he replied. The expression on his face told me he had something more he wanted to say.

"Is everything alright?" I inquired.

He hesitantly began to tell us that he had overheard others talking about him. Alex shared with Kido about the time he had been challenged with a similar situation.

"I've learned that words have the power to leave a good mark or an ugly stain on our hearts. Sometimes the hurt is not visible right away, just like sin. It slowly spreads, causing a path of suffering," Alex explained. "I had a friend once who spread gossip about me to others on the basketball team." Alex leaned over licking the dripping cone he held.

"What did you do about it?" Kido asked.

"Well, I couldn't stop him. But, what I could do was be careful to guard my own tongue and stay out of the path of the gossip. The old saying, 'sticks and stones will break my bones, but names will never hurt me,' isn't always true. Our words can make a big difference in someone's life. The most important things we can do, Kido, is to pray and forgive." Alex reached over and patted him on the shoulder.

Before we left to go home, Alex led us in prayer. "Lord, help us not to gossip. Help us to be a blessing to others with our words. Amen."

We sang hymns and spiritual songs all the way home in the car. The pleasure of the sweet ice cream cones was evident by the drippings on our chins and shirts. Walking up the porch to the house, I reminded Alex, "Duck your head. Be careful not to get any of those pesty worms on your clothes; they'll stain!"

"Thanks for the reminder, Mother. And I'll sure be careful with my words, too. I'd much rather make ice cream stains on my shirt than make stains of unkind words on someone's heart any day!"

The cankerworm, or inchworm, is a caterpillar of a moth. Cankerworms spin down on a strand of long, silken thread they discharge from their mouths. Their fluorescent green bodies drop onto people, cars, and picnic areas leaving dark brown spots making them destructive nuisances.

Discussion

What did Jesus do when people talked behind his back? How does the Bible say to respond if someone gossips about you? How is gossip harmful, and who does it harm? How would you encourage someone injured by gossip? What songs do you sing when you ride in the car?

Scripture

"He who loves a pure heart and whose speech is gracious will have the king for his friend." Proverbs 22:11

"Avoid godless chatter, because those who indulge in it will become more and more ungodly." 2 Timothy 2:16

"Let the word of Christ dwell in you richly as you teach and admonish one another with all wisdom, and as you sing psalms, hymns and spiritual songs with gratitude in your hearts to God." Colossians 3:16

Song

"Nothing But The Blood Of Jesus" and "Whiter Than Snow"

Application

Read James chapter three. Make a list of all the adjectives that describe the tongue. Discuss what you find. Write a blessing on an index card and place it on the table at mealtime for family or guest. Encourage one another to sing hymns and spiritual songs when tempted to speak unkindly of others. Plan an evening to make ice cream floats, sundaes, or Cups O' Dirt.

Idiom

A penny for your thoughts means to tell what is on your mind.

Prayer

Ask the Lord to show you if you have hurt someone with your words. If you have hurt someone, ask the Lord's forgiveness and then go to that person and apologize.

Chapter 29

Trash Talk

*"I will extol the LORD at all times; his
praise will always be on my lips."*

PSALM 34:1

In the summer evenings, the guys in the neighborhood would gather at the camp to play basketball. The families lined up around the court to cheer on their favorite team. If you were anywhere near the court when they played, you would get a chance to play, too. Tonight there was a visitor at the camp who wanted to join in on the action.

"Jump on in," Alex shouted, waving his arms until he had attracted the guest's attention. "We can always use one more body." Alex loved playing basketball, and would get a game started whenever he could. The court was full of action that night. Sweaty players knocked elbows, shoulders, and calves. At one point, I saw Alex and the young guest exchange words on the court, but I did not give it much thought.

The evening passed quickly. Before we knew it, the automatic lights on the court shut off, and it was time to go home. We grabbed our lawn chairs and water bottles and strolled up the hill. After Alex cooled down with a shower and some lemonade, we decided to take out the trash.

"Come on, Mom. Let's walk down to the dumpster." With a flashlight tucked under his arm and a trash bag in each of our hands, we headed out the door. It was about ten o' clock, and the only light we saw was from our neighbor's porch illuminating small portions of the inky night.

We walked down the hill to the dumpster. The only sounds we heard were the crunching of gravel under our footsteps and the swishing of our heavy bags. Alex opened the large, metal dumpster with a "one, two, three, plunk!" The trash landed perfectly in the dumpster with a swoosh—just like a slam dunk. "Good shot, Alex, especially in the dark!" The heavy, metal top came down with a crash.

As we walked back up the hill, I asked, "How was the game tonight?"

"*Right off the bat*, the guy that was guarding me was talking trash on the court trying to make me lose my focus," said Alex. "I tried to ignore him and guard my own words."

"I'm so sorry, Alex. It looked like everything was just fine from where I was standing."

"Things aren't always what they seem, Mother. But, I was grateful for the chance to play basketball tonight," he said candidly.

As we walked home, we noticed a cat ahead of us crossing the road in front of our house. He seemed to be walking kind of funny—maybe even limping. As we got closer, Alex turned his flashlight in the animal's direction, and then immediately turned it off.

"Mom, it's not a cat. It's a skunk! Shhh, quiet, tiptoe. Don't let him hear us," Alex directed. *How do I tiptoe on gravel?* I thought. Alex paused, held my arm, and whispered, "Freeze, Mom. Don't move. We don't want to startle him." We stood still, not moving a muscle.

We could see his little body strut up toward the house, stopping and snooping around the bushes along the way. We tried to keep the skunk in our view, but he disappeared into the darkness. Thinking it was safe, we darted across the road and hid behind our car. We wanted to be sure we would not cross his path again.

"I don't want to get any closer, Alex, until we're sure he's gone for good." With my back pressed against the car, I could hear my heartbeat. We waited patiently to make sure the inquisitive visitor did not reappear.

We could still smell strong traces of his stinky little body even though he was a good distance away. Our eyes were fixed in his direction, watching for any movement in the brush. Suddenly, he appeared from the shadowy bushes. The familiar white stripe on his back swayed back and forth as he hobbled toward us. We both froze, not wanting to excite the skunk.

"Alex, I have an idea. Grab a stick and throw it into the bushes down the hill. Hopefully that will distract him enough to let us escape!"

Alex inched toward a broken branch lying in the middle of the road, picked it up, and hurled it toward a bush. When the skunk heard the curious sound, he turned away just long enough for us to scurry away. *Whew, That was a close call!* We cautiously ran the rest of the way home without getting sprayed.

Once we were safely inside the house, we talked about our unexpected encounter that night, thankful for the great escape. It was a vivid reminder that we should pay close attention to our surroundings.

"Mom, I had no idea that was a skunk on the road in front of us. It looked just like a cat."

"Let's remember that things are not always like they appear, Son. It's wise to be discerning about people, places, and things."

"Yes, and now I appreciate even more the value of encouraging words," he added. "Trash talk is for the dumpster, not for the basketball court!"

It is comforting to know that God is always with us, even when we don't see trouble around us. I was prayerful that Alex would remember these lessons the next time he played basketball.

> *Skunks have small, short legs that make them walk with a slow, rolling gait. Skunks raise their tails when startled as a warning to their predators. Skunks have poor eyesight, but they can smell and hear well. Skunks have been known to approach people who are standing still. If you are approached by a skunk, slowly move away in the opposite direction.*

Discussion

Why is it important to choose wise companions? How has discernment helped you avoid trouble? How would you respond if confronted with unwholesome words? When is it helpful to be silent? How can praising the Lord help us overcome the temptation to return unkind words?

Scripture

"He who walks with the wise grows wise, but a companion of fools suffers harm." Proverbs 13:20

"Do not let any unwholesome talk come out of your mouths, but only what is helpful for building others up according to their needs, that it may benefit those who listen." Ephesians 4:29

"Let your conversation be always full of grace, seasoned with salt, so that you may know how to answer everyone." Colossians 4:6

"Prove all things; hold fast that which is good." 1 Thessalonians 5:21

Song

"Leaning On The Everlasting Arms" and "Awesome God"

Application

Choose a chore to do alongside your child. Teach him to pay close attention to details. Plan a neighborhood trash pickup day; serve lemonade afterward. Start a Bible reading group (e.g., read the Bible through in a year). Include a time of praise and worship at your gathering. Allow time for a basketball game, ping pong, or board game.

Idiom

Right off the bat means immediately.
Close call means a narrow escape.

Prayer

Thank the Lord for your Godly friendships. Ask Him to help you choose encouraging words and deeds.

Chapter 30

Tuxie

"When words are many, sin is not absent,
but he who holds his tongue is wise."

Proverbs 10:19

Friday was our busiest day of the week at the camp. A long chore list waited for me on the kitchen counter. The phone rang, and the voice of my supervisor kindly asked, "Could you please get some gas for the tractor today?" I quickly agreed in a rushed tone, trying to get off the phone.

"Good morning, Mom," said Alex, stretching and yawning his way from his room.

"Good morning, Son, how did you sleep last night?"

"Great, I was *out like a light*," he answered. He slowly walked over to the couch, but I quickly halted his next step.

"Hold on. I need you to get dressed and hurry down to the barn to get the gas can for me, please. We have a group coming tonight, the field has to be mowed by evening, and I have to get some gasoline."

"Sure, Mom. I'll run and get it right away." In no time he was out the door. I stood beside the car, waiting for him to return.

"Here you go, Mom. Sorry it took so long, but it was in the shed, not the barn," he said, sensing that I was ready to go.

"That's alright, Alex. I have to run now. See you in a little bit."

"What time will you be back?" he asked.

"As soon as I can, if this list doesn't get any longer." The words were out of my mouth before I realized how sharp they sounded. Alex headed out to do his morning chores.

My speech had been abrupt that morning, and I was already wishing I could take back some of the words I had spoken. As I pulled out of the driveway, I saw a few of the other ladies from the camp standing by the mailboxes. *No time to stop and talk right now*, I murmured. *There is so much to get done.* Smiling insincerely, I carefully drove by them, but my friend Jennifer stepped out in front of the car and stopped me.

"Hi there, what's the hurry?" she inquired with a friendly smile.

"I've got a lot to do today—gotta run. See you later." I waved at the others and rolled up the window. I hurried to get my errands done.

Alex met me in the driveway when I arrived back home with the gasoline. "How's your day going, Mom?" he kindly asked.

"Well, I'm checking gasoline off my list. But I realize there's something else that I need to keep a check on, and that's my tongue." Overlooking my confession, Alex took the gasoline can to the young man who was waiting to do the mowing, then returned to his chores. The list in my hand was dwindling as I checked off each completed task. The mad rush was almost behind me, and the afternoon was coming to an end.

Alex seemed a little quiet that evening. After dinner, I asked if he wanted to take a walk. We both agreed that walking would be a good way to unwind. It started out as a quiet stroll.

"How was your day, Alex?" I asked.

"It was a little hectic," he admitted. The trail we walked was crowded with rocks of all sizes. It took some effort to walk over the rocks and yet keep our eyes on the path ahead of us.

Suddenly, a long-eared jack rabbit dashed out of nowhere. It streaked across our path like a bolt of lightning. "Did you see that?" we both said at the same time. All we could see were long legs bounding past us. It landed right behind one of the big rocks.

"I barely saw him. Did you get a good look at him?" I asked Alex.

"No, he shot by like a cannonball!" he answered.

We slowed our pace as we walked up the path. In a matter of seconds, the rabbit reappeared, leaping from rock to rock until he had made his way up the hill. All we could see in the far-off distance was his dark, buff-colored fur and his peppered black ears.

"Wow, he was quick!" I said. We looked at each other, stunned.

"I didn't know rabbits could hop so high or so fast!" said Alex.

On our way home, after the excitement had worn off, the encounter with the long-eared jack rabbit made me think back on the day's events. It felt like the day had gone by so quickly, and I began again to question some of my actions.

I remembered that I had spoken sharply to my supervisor on the phone. My speech with Alex had been careless and hasty. With the speed of a jack rabbit, my words had spilled out, and I could never take any of them back. My attitude to the ladies at the mailbox that morning was camouflaged with a smile, but my conscience told me differently. I had missed the opportunity to say something kind to them.

First, I went to Alex. "Alex, I am sorry that I was sharp with my words today. My attitude was not pleasing or honoring to you or the Lord. Will you please forgive me?"

"Yes, Mother. I forgive you."

"Thank you, Alex. Let's pray. Lord Jesus, forgive me for my quick tongue. Help me slow down and guard my speech. Please, help me think about what I am going to say before I say it. In Jesus' name, Amen."

We often spotted the long-eared jack rabbit on our walks. We would see him hopping across the hills, darting between the big rocks. We named him "Tuxie" because his black-spotted tail and ears resembled a tuxedo. His quick leaps across the horizon reminded us that once our words are out of our mouths, they are gone forever. When we were tempted to speak quickly or unkindly, we reminded each other, "Slow down and remember Tuxie!"

Sometimes, stressful situations make it more challenging to restrain our words. We have all had circumstances that reveal our need to think before we speak. We are naturally tempted to make quick judgments and react hastily. Therefore, the Bible exhorts us to take special care concerning our tongue.

The Jackrabbit can run as fast as forty-five miles per hour. Jackrabbits are powerful jumpers. A twenty-inch adult can jump five feet high and leap twenty feet in a single bound. Jackrabbits are strict vegetarians. They have excellent hearing from ears five inches long.

Discussion

Where in this story were there missed opportunities to be a blessing? How does this story encourage you to "think before you speak"? What steps can you take to become a better listener? How can you guard from having a sharp tongue? How does the Bible say to make amends?

Scripture

"Does not the ear test words as the tongue tastes food?" Job 12:11

"My tongue will speak of your righteousness and of your praises all day long." Psalm 35:28

"He who answers before listening—that is his folly and his shame." Proverbs 18:13

"Out of the same mouth come praise and cursing. My brothers, this should not be." James 3:10

Song

"O For A Thousand Tongues To Sing" and "Blessed Be Your Name"

Activity

Play the game "Red Light, Green Light."

Application

Create a power list of positive words A–Z, to encourage others (e.g., awesome, blessed, courage, delight, efficient, glorious, happy). Post the list in a central location to encourage positive speech. Record your conversations with your siblings as you go about your day. Listen and learn which areas of communication need improvement.

Idiom

Out like a light means to sleep very soundly.

Prayer

Pray and ask the Lord to help you be a blessing to others with your words.

Chapter 31

Brotherly Love

"Be devoted to one another in brotherly love.
Honor one another above yourselves."

ROMANS 12:10

Valor was our house guest for the summer. He was part of the Korean mission team visiting America to learn about homeschooling. The team stayed at the retreat center where we lived.

He had arrived in the US speaking very little English. During Valor's three month visit, he became part of our family. Alex called him "Brother." Alex was glad to have a study partner as well as a buddy to help with the chores around the camp.

"Will you guys please grab the buckets and bleach? And don't forget the brooms." I, too, was happy for the extra help. We piled in the golf cart and headed up the hill to scrub the outside pavilion floor for the upcoming retreat.

"Why don't you and Valor move the benches out on the lawn while I hook up the hose? Teamwork!" I exclaimed. One by one, we moved the heavy seats so that we could wash the cement floor. Working in the Texas summer heat was scorching, so the occasional breezes that made it up the hill were a welcome relief. Working outside was wonderful, no matter what job we were doing.

"Come on, Valor, let's start over here." Alex instructed. He showed Valor how to get down on the floor and scrub the spots with a hard brush. Grime turned to gleam as we cleaned off spilled drinks, old chewing gum, and other foreign substances. The pavilion was quite large, and it would take the three of us to get the job done.

Alex and Valor worked on the open area, scrubbing the hard surface. It was great to see these two young men working together. They represented the next godly generation; this thought made my work seem lighter. Valor moved about from one side of the pavilion to the other, distracted by all the new surroundings. You could see the wonder on his face.

"Come on, Valor. Over here," Alex directed.

"Alex, how are things going?" I asked, wanting to encourage him.

"Well, Mom, to tell you the truth, he's *dragging his feet*. I've covered twice the area he has. At this pace, we'll be here all day." Alex was visibly frustrated.

"Alex, Valor has never done work like this before. Let's try to practice patience."

"You're right, Mom. I'll try to be more patient," Alex replied, and returned to Valor's side.

"Let's put a little *elbow grease* into it, Valor," Alex said, helping him.

We broke for a quick drink of water and sat down under a shade tree. After quenching our thirst, we resumed our laborious job. My job was to be the tail-gaiter. That is, I followed behind the guys with a hose rinsing the areas they had scrubbed. I received the benefit of feeling the cold water splash across my bare feet.

"Valor, you missed a spot here," I heard Alex point out. A few minutes later, Alex walked over and pulled me aside.

"Mom, look at Valor now. He's sitting down over there while we're working."

I walked over to give Valor a word of encouragement. He was sitting down on the wet cement. "What are you up to, Valor? Are you learning anything new?" I asked, hoping to be a blessing.

"Look at this furry thing I found. I've never seen one of these in Korea." Valor was sitting down with a stick, playing with a small furry-legged insect. Indeed, he was discovering something new.

"That's a caterpillar," I said, stooping down to take a closer look. "You'll see many bugs here in Texas that you won't see in Korea. And all our bugs here are big!"

"Look how slowly he crawls," Valor said, with wonder.

Out of the corner of my eye, I saw Alex scrubbing away, gazing over at us while we chatted about the discovery. Remembering a conversation we had earlier, I realized Valor had never worked in big, outdoor spaces like this before. He lived in a high-rise community in Korea. I walked over to remind Alex of this while still encouraging both of them to get the job done.

"Alex, remember this is new to Valor. He isn't experienced with this type of work. Let's allow the Lord to teach all of us patience." I realized how very blessed we were to have this opportunity. Working together was a gift from the Lord.

"Look at all the legs on the worm!" Valor said, as he walked over with the caterpillar dangling from the stick. I put the hose down and turned the water off. I motioned for the guys to take a time out.

"Come on, Alex, Valor—let's look at the caterpillar."

"Valor, do you see that all the parts of the caterpillar work together to make him move? He has a head, a body, and many legs. He needs every part of his body to work together. We are all part of this job and need to support each other as we work. When the caterpillar matures, he will become a beautiful butterfly. One day, you and Alex will mature into Godly, young men."

"Valor, you can put the caterpillar in that extra bucket over there. You're welcome to take him home when we've finished work, and put him in a jar." This settled his interest. He and Alex walked away excitedly, retrieving the old, plastic container.

I was grateful for the time out that Valor's curiosity provoked. Alex was challenged to be patient. I was challenged in having to see the work done in more time than expected. Valor learned about caterpillars. And we all finished the job a bit wiser.

"Good job, Brother," said Alex, as he gave Valor a big "high five."

Caterpillars are ravenous eaters with strong jaws, spending most of their time eating leaves. A caterpillar's first meal is its own eggshell. Caterpillars have 4,000 muscles, 248 of which are in their head (compared with humans who have only 629 muscles).

Discussion

What does "brotherly love" mean to you? How can you better demonstrate patience at home or while you are working? What are the benefits of "teamwork"? Who are your teammates (e.g., siblings, Sunday School class, soccer team)? What are some ways you have experienced the Lord's patience and kindness?

Scripture

"How good and pleasant it is when brothers live together in unity!" Psalm 133:1

"Why do you look at the speck of sawdust in your brother's eye and pay no attention to the plank in your own eye?" Matthew 7:3

"Love is patient, love is kind. It does not envy, it does not boast, it is not proud. It is not rude, it is not self-seeking, it is not easily angered, it keeps no record of wrongs. Love does not delight in evil but rejoices with the truth. It always protects, always trusts, always hopes, always perseveres. Love never fails." 1 Corinthians 13: 4–8a

Song

"The Butterfly Song (If I Were A Butterfly)" and "They Will Know We Are Christians By Our Love"

Application

Plan a family work day. Write a catchy family-team slogan to sing while you work (e.g., "Whatever the weather, we'll all work together."). Craft a sign for your study or schoolroom that reads: TEAMWORK. Study the life cycle of a butterfly or moth. Children love to help wash the car, driveway, or deck. Cool off with homemade popsicles.

Idiom

Dragging his feet means slowly doing what you do not want to do.
Elbow grease means enthusiastic, hard manual labor.

Prayer

Pray and ask the Lord to help you be a blessing to those you work beside.

Chapter 32

Fix Your Eyes

"Man looks at the outward appearance,
but the Lord looks at the heart."

1 SAMUEL 16:7B

If I told you that there was a skunk around my house, you might think that it was no big deal. Or, maybe you would consider it a nuisance, especially for someone who was living in the country for the first time. Trying to get others to understand what it is like being plagued by a skunk is not an easy thing. I wondered why, out of all the residences at the camp, the smelly, little critter hung around our house.

Attempts to defend our house from the assaults of our furry foe continued. There were many nights that we found ourselves awakened by the foul aroma that seeped through the cracks in the windows and doors. Alex had worn a beaten path around the perimeter of the house, checking night and day for any signs or tracks of tiny paws. The distraction of the skunk was ongoing and demanding. We were hoping that he might soon lose interest in our house and find new amusement somewhere else, but the skunk remained.

A day in April started out as one of my usual Saturday mornings—with an outing to the grocery store. Little did I realize that it would turn into another stinky situation. Bidding farewell to Alex, who was mowing the lawn, I set out for the market.

In the store, minding my own business, out of the corner of my eye, I saw a young boy staring at me as I strolled down the aisle. I assumed he was glancing at something on the shelf beside me. I did not think much of it, and, turning the corner, I walked down the next aisle.

As I continued to shop, I noticed glares from the other people who were walking by me. As time went on, I could sense more and more people looking my way. Feelings of uneasiness slowly crept over me, for it felt as if all eyes were on me as I walked through the store.

It seemed odd to me that I was attracting so much attention. *That's funny,* I thought. *People are usually pretty focused on the list in their hand or in their head. They are there for a purpose, after all.*

As I leaned over the cooler in the meat department, I glanced to one side and saw a young girl giggling in her mother's ear. Immediately the verse, "A cheerful heart is good medicine" (Proverbs 17:22) popped into my head. *Oh, how sweet,* I said to myself as I smiled, admiring their tender exchange. I continued on my way.

When I finished my shopping, I headed to the front of the store, and found the checkout lines flooded with customers. Spotting a shorter line at the customer service counter, I waded my way through the mass of people and stood in the line with my arms folded.

Right away, the woman in front of me turned around and looked directly at me, but she did not say a word. *Do I look like someone she knows?* I asked myself. The tension in the air was thickening.

The man in the very front of the line turned around after he checked out his groceries, and walked right past me, staring as if he was disturbed with me for some reason. Was this my imagination? Then I heard someone behind me whisper, "Someone smells like a skunk!" When I heard those words, *my world stood still.* The word, "skunk, skunk, skunk," echoed boldly in my mind.

Suddenly, I realized people were talking about me! Oh, how awful—I smelled like a skunk! My stomach knotted up and my knees went limp as noodles. I had to stand there, in line, with three people still ahead of me. Never did I imagine that my clothes stunk. No wonder people were glaring at me when I walked through the store.

I stunk like a skunk—it rang in my head. By the time I made it up to the counter, the cashier looked like she could not wait to get me out of the store. Quickly snatching my bags, I fled to the car in tears, gasping with each breath. I drove home, shaken up by the ordeal at the store. I was considered "undesirable" simply by the way I smelled, a result of the intruder who lived under my house.

I ran into the house, took a shower, and then threw my clothes in the trash. I sat down at the kitchen table trying to calm my nerves after this embarrassing ordeal. After that incident at the store, I realized how awful others must feel when people make fun of them. *Had I ever treated anyone that way?* I asked myself.

The Bible tells us that man looks on the outward appearance, but Jesus looks at what is in our hearts. This experience made me more aware of how we judge others by outward appearances. God showed me how important it is to demonstrate His love to others no matter what they look like or even what they smell like. My prayer that night was that my eyes would always be fixed on Jesus.

Skunk musk is one of the longest lasting odors in nature. The powerful odor can linger from several days to several months. Skunk spray can temporarily blind an attacker and burn its eyes, but it does not cause permanent damage. Skunks are sensitive, non-agressive animals, but they have little fear when confronted by an opponent.

Discussion

What does it mean to judge another person? How would you respond if someone laughed at you? What would you do to comfort someone who was being scorned? What does God's Word say about forgiveness? What does it mean to have "eyes like Jesus"?

Scripture

"But my eyes are fixed on you, O Sovereign LORD; in you I take refuge." Psalm 141:8a

"For a man's ways are in full view of the LORD, and he examines all his paths." Proverbs 5:21

"The eye is the lamp of the body. If your eyes are good, your whole body will be full of light." Matthew 6:22

"Do to others as you would have them do to you." Luke 6:31

"Let us fix our eyes on Jesus, the author and perfecter of our faith." Hebrews 12:2a

Song

"Turn Your Eyes Upon Jesus" and "Open The Eyes Of My Heart"

Application

Draw pictures of the things on which the Bible tells us to direct our eyes (e.g., heavens, hills, God's Word). Explain your picture. Play "I Spy." Pick an object that everyone can see, and say its color. Have the other players guess what object you spy. Play "Fix Your Eyes." Stare your opponent in their eyes until one of you blinks or laughs. Onlookers can use words or sounds as distractions.

Idiom

My world stood still means to remain fixed or motionless.

Prayer

Ask Jesus to fix your eyes to see others as He sees them.

Chapter 33

Steering

*"Trust in the Lord and do good; dwell in
the land and enjoy safe pasture."*

PSALM 37:3

Our neighbors had asked us to feed their horses while they were away for the weekend. This allowed us the opportunity to enjoy an extra stretch of relaxation while admiring the uniqueness of the Texas countryside.

"Hold on, here we go. Youch! Here comes the last cattle guard, Alex, brace yourself," I warned.

"That sure was a rough ride, Mom," he grinned. "But where are the cattle?"

"It looks like there aren't any cattle here, just a few horses," I laughed.

Alex led the way from the car to the paddock, tromping through the mud that was left behind by the afternoon thunderstorm. Inside the paddock stood a small horse barn with two beautiful quarter horses peering out of the top gate of their stalls. They were neighing and snorting, *chomping at the bit*, waiting for their evening meal.

Inside the fenced-in paddock was a flat-bed trailer stacked high with hay. The sweet, strong smell of the hay made me think that the horses' mouths must always water having to stare at the scrumptious hay all day. Once we were inside the paddock, Alex climbed on top of the hay stack.

"Mom, come on up here!"

"No thank you," I said, "I'm just fine down here." I walked over to the barn to pet the hungry horses.

"Mom, how am I going to get this hay out?" He stood triumphantly, looking down like a conquering mountain climber.

"What do you mean?" I walked over to the trailer and saw that the hay was wrapped tightly with bailing twine. Looking around for something to cut it with, I could not find anything that would do. Feeding horses was a brand new adventure for city folk like us. With one big snap, Alex popped the twine with his bare hands and it fell to the ground.

"You're so strong, Alex!" I called, beaming up at him.

Alex began dropping the large flakes of hay off the trailer. I picked up the flakes of hay and tossed them into the horses' stalls. Their chomping let us know that they had already forgotten about us. Alex stood atop the haystack, looking to and fro across the horizon.

"Mom, it looks like there's a big cow over there in the field," he pointed. I walked closer to the trailer to try and see what he was talking about.

"It sure is—a really big cow!" I answered. Alex reached his hand down to help me climb up the heap so that I could get a better look. By now the large, lanky, quadruped was closer to us.

"Mother, look at that. The horns on that cow are so big he can barely walk. They must be four feet wide. It looks like his head is going to bob right off!" The big cow walked slowly, moping his way across the open field.

"It looks like he's coming over here," said Alex. Our neighbor had only told us about her prized horses, but she never mentioned any cattle. The cow with the huge horns had picked up his pace and was headed our way. By now we were both *wound up* and feeling the excitement of our Western adventure. Alex tugged on my arm to alert me.

"Look over there, Mom. There's two more big cows headed right this way."

"Alex, I suspect they smell the hay."

Now three longhorns were headed in our direction, and we were suddenly outnumbered. We stayed on top of the trailer, watching those three pokey, heavy-headed cattle meander across the field. Before we knew it, like a bull's-eye, there was a stream of longhorns headed straight for the stall.

"Look, there's another one," Alex counted. "Behind that tree," he pointed. "And another one—ten, eleven, twelve," he counted. He stopped counting at thirteen. There were thirteen big Texas Longhorns coming our way. They slowly made a line around the fence. By now, I was glad to be safe on top of the haystack. The cattle stood staring up at us.

"Mom, they want the hay," Alex whispered.

"Yes, and I want to get out of here," I nervously murmured. We remained on top of the haystack watching all thirteen longhorns dawdle in front of the large gate. The pathway out from the paddock to the car was blocked. In the meantime, the two horses were chomping away on their meal, never looking up even once.

"Mom, how are we going to get out of here?"

"Let's stop for a second and think, Son. No, better yet, let's pray. Heavenly Father, we thank you that we can always have faith in you. We ask for your guidance and safety from this haystack to our car. Amen."

"I know, Mom," Alex suggested, "I'll give them some hay." That sounded like a good idea. Slipping away without first feeding them did not seem possible. The big cows looked very serious about their business.

"This is what I'll do," Alex explained. "I'll take some hay and jump the fence to the other side of the paddock. Then, I'll lead them away from the gate." Wrenching my hands I listened to Alex explain his plan.

"I'll trickle a trail of hay away from the gate, and "steer" them right back into the open field."

"Oh, what a great idea, Alex. That makes perfect sense!"

"You wait here, Mother, you'll be safe." He jumped from the trailer.

My goal was to keep the cows looking my direction and away from Alex. Standing on top of the haystack, waving my arms I chanted, "Yippie kai yay, yippie kai yo, get along little dogie." Alex eagerly waded through the mud to the opposite side of the paddock clutching a big armload of hay.

"Yippie kai yay, yippie kai yo, get along little dogie," I sang, earnestly trying to keep the cows' attention.

Alex turned back and yelled, "Where's the doggie, Mom?"

"Dogie, not doggie. Dogie means stray calf in cowboy language," I informed him. He chuckled my way with a grin.

I was able to keep the longhorns distracted long enough for Alex to safely lay a pathway of hay away from the paddock. Once that was accomplished, Alex climbed safely back into the paddock. We patiently watched the longhorns, one by one, turn and follow Alex's brilliant trail of hay, eating their way back to the open field.

Once the cows had left the area and returned to the pasture, we were able to safely make a dash for the car. Driving away, we found the bumpy ride over the cattle guard to be a welcome annoyance, as we watched the longhorns lumbering off into the horizon.

"With a little bit of hay and a little bit of faith, those longhorns changed direction," Alex said with a sigh. "Thank you, Lord, for leading us to safety," we both prayed with heartfelt offering.

The Word of God is like that, too. It leads us, feeds us, and steers us in the right direction. The Lord leads us to safe pastures.

The Texas Longhorn is a "heart-healthy" beef cattle native to Texas. From tip to tip, its long, twisted horns have grown up to a record ten feet. Texas Longhorns eat cactus for water, including the thorns. The Texas Longhorn is a symbol of the Old West.

Discussion

Who is leading you to be like Jesus? Who is the faithful Shepherd, and how does He lead us? How does faith help you when you are faced with an unexpected trial or hardship? How does reading the Bible direct your path? Where would you lead or direct someone who was in a difficult situation?

From the Bible

"The Lord is my shepherd, I shall not be in want. He makes me lie down in green pastures, he leads me beside quiet waters, he restores my soul. He guides me in paths of righteousness for his name's sake." Psalm 23:1–3

"For in the gospel a righteousness from God is revealed, a righteousness that is by faith from first to last, just as it is written: 'The righteous will live by faith.'" Romans 1:17

"And without faith it is impossible to please God, because anyone who comes to him must believe that he exists and that he rewards those who earnestly seek him." Hebrews 11:6

Song

"Go Tell It On The Mountain" and "Savior Like a Shepherd Lead Us"

Application

Sketch a trail of God's love from the birth of Jesus to the Cross (Bible stories from Bethlehem to Calvary). Explain what you have drawn. Make labels naming all the ways God's Word leads, feeds, and meets your needs. Draw a picture of a haystack, and paste your labels onto it. Play the game "Follow the Leader."

Idiom

Chomping at the bit means showing impatience or eagerness.
Wound up means excited or stirred up.

Prayer

Thank God for the beautiful animals He has created and for leading us in paths that are righteous.

Chapter 34

Walls Came Tumbling Down

"But thanks be to God, who always leads
us in triumphal procession in Christ
and through us spreads everywhere the
fragrance of the knowledge of him."

2 CORINTHIANS 2:14

There would soon be a vacant house at the camp, and we were told that we could move there. This was an answer to prayer. Moving to a new location would be a welcomed solution to the two-year skirmish with the skunks. This conflict was soon to end, or so we thought.

The empty house sat high on a hill not far from the other residences. When we visited the house, we first noticed the two tall pink crepe myrtle bushes. As we walked around the yard admiring the big beautiful oak trees, my mind imagined all the fellowship that we could have there. We went inside to inspect the home.

"Let's check out my bedroom," Alex said as he wandered down the hallway.

He eagerly opened the first door he found. "Come and look, Mother. This room already has a built-in desk." His smile showed that he was glad to have his own study space.

Moving day came quickly with many expectations. The new location was only a half a mile from where we were already living, so I assumed that this would be an easy change. We were able to move almost everything in one day. That first night we slept on the floor.

When I awoke early the next morning, I thought I smelled a foul odor. *No, it can't be*, I told myself. Yet, suspicions gnawed at me. Indeed, I smelled something that was a little too familiar. I convinced myself that it was nothing, just that the house had been sitting empty for a while. Then, Alex approached me with a concerned look on his face.

"Mom, I think there's a skunk under the house. Come here to the back bedroom and see if you can smell it; it's really strong."

"Imagine that. That little fellow followed us here," I sadly replied. Alex's face looked strained with disappointment.

"Alex, if indeed it is a skunk, we have to press on through this trial. I don't understand it, but we have to believe that the Lord gave us this new place to live, and we can trust Him."

We bowed our heads and prayed, "Father, please give us a contented heart and courage for any trial we face here at this new house. Amen."

Our camp neighbors laughed and joked with us, saying we wasted our time worrying about skunks. To our surprise, there were those who were able to live peaceably alongside this very unique animal.

Within a few days, we were certain that there was indeed a skunk living beneath our house. Skunks sleep during the day, but all it took was the sound of our footsteps down the hallway to wake him and cause him to spray. The strong smell forced us to de-skunk the house.

Immediately, Alex set a trap outside a window at the corner of the house. He made a trail of white, pasty flour leading to the cage. Paw prints in the flour would be evidence of his visit. Next, Alex set some peanut butter in the trap. We read somewhere that skunks like peanut butter.

Posting ourselves in the corner of the living room, we waited with the lights out. With our flashlights in our laps, we sat back in our seats contemplating the mission before us. We were hoping to get a peek at the mysterious, black and white nomad.

"Mom, this is a lot of fun. Think of all the memories we're making."

"That's right, Alex—smelly memories, too!"

We took turns watching for the persistent follower. Alex nestled in a chair over in the corner of the room asleep. There was an island of cabinets in the center of the kitchen. Keeping a close watch out the window while I was trying to stay awake, a favorite Bible story came to mind. *What a great idea,* I thought to myself. *I'll march around this island like Jericho and pray that little skunk right into the trap! That will keep me alert.* And that is exactly what I did. I marched around the cabinets praying and praising the Lord—trusting Him in this present circumstance.

"Alex, wake up. It's your turn to watch." I gently shook him from his sleep and explained the marching plans.

"Keep your chin up; march and pray and wait, march and pray and wait!"

Then we prayed, "Lord, please give us courage for this night. Amen." This strenuous vigil lasted until daybreak. The next morning Alex went outside to check the trap and found paw prints in the flour.

"Mom, this little fellow *out-skunked* us! Why do you think we are the only ones here at the camp that are bothered by skunks?"

"Alex, I have no idea. But one thing I do know, God will see us through this ordeal. He is always with us." He baited the cage again with his newest skunk-luring recipe of sardines and hot sauce, hoping to capture the crafty varmint.

That evening, while on "skunk watch," I remembered all the ways the Lord had been faithful to our family. Alex was fast asleep as I marched and prayed around the kitchen cabinets. Lifting my hands in praise to the Lord, I sang, "Oh victory in Jesus, my Savior forever…"

Then, suddenly, the most pronounced wave of skunk musk I think I have ever smelled seeped into the house. I dashed over to the window and turned on my flashlight. *Oh my, there he is!* I gently shook Alex, not to scare him.

"Alex, the skunk is here!" Startled but alert, he jumped to his feet.

"I thought I was dreaming," he shouted. "Yahoo! We got 'em, he's in the cage!"

With our flashlights pointed out the window, we saw the huge skunk trapped in the cage with his tail sticking straight up in the air, spraying like a squirt gun. The smell came through the house like a tidal wave. Finally this little critter's wrath would not pester us any longer. The territorial conflict had come to an end; our daily routines would no longer provoke this smelly reaction to waking the skunk from his sleep.

We watched by the window waiting for the skunk to calm down and stop spraying. He finally did calm down, but we decided to leave him there until morning so that we could call the animal rescue to come and get him. Tired, smelly, and excited that the vigil had ended, we rolled on the floor, laughing with relief.

Days later, we finally moved the rest of our things into our new home. God gave us many happy, memorable times of worship and fellowship while we lived there. The skunk trial made us stronger in the Lord. The Lord taught us that He is faithful to see us though to the other side of any stinky situation. God is our Victor!

Skunks are nocturnal and are rarely seen during the day. Skunks will occasionally roam in daylight if they are either sick or moving their young or if their den is upset. Skunks often move from den to den because of their nomadic tendencies. Skunks are solitary animals and live most of their lives alone.

Discussion

How can unpleasant circumstances teach us to trust God? What are ways we can demonstrate our trust in God while we wait for Him to deliver us in our trial (e.g., worship, seeking God's will, service)? Why is it so important to remain grateful during those "unchangeable" circumstances? Why should we obey God first before we understand?

Scripture

"Have I not commanded you? Be strong and courageous. Do not be terrified; do not be discouraged, for the LORD your God will be with you wherever you go." Joshua 1:9

"The seventh time around, when the priests sounded the trumpet blast, Joshua commanded the people, 'Shout! For the LORD has given you the city!'" Joshua 6:16

"Not only so, but we also rejoice in our sufferings, because we know that suffering produces perseverance; perseverance, character; and character, hope." Romans 5:3–4

Song

"Joshua Fought The Battle At Jericho" and "Victory In Jesus"

Application

Read Joshua 6. Role-play, "Fear not, march and wait." Make an island out of a box or table. March around it, proclaiming the faithfulness of the Lord. Give a loud shout! Use a ram's horn if you have one or a small instrument. (Drum, tambourine, pan and spoon, or whistle). Craft a scripture mural of verses which proclaim your family's mission statement (e.g., "But as for me and my household, we will serve the Lord." Joshua 24:15).

Idiom

Out-skunked means to be out-witted.

Prayer

Thank the Lord for His presence during the good times as well as the hard times.

Chapter 35

Under Cover

*"We wait in hope for the LORD; he
is our help and our shield."*

PSALM 33:20

"Alex, hurry, please! You grab the volleyballs and rakes, and I'll latch down the windows. Let's take cover here and wait it out. We don't have time to make it home."

The wind was picking up speed and the dark clouds were rushing overhead. Out of nowhere a storm was brewing. The recreation hall was the closest and safest place to wait out the summer rainstorm. The chores outside would have to wait. There was plenty of work to do inside until the showers passed.

"How about a game of ping pong until the rain stops?" Alex asked.

"First, let's sweep the floor, and then we can play."

"Okay, Mom, I know. Work first, and then play."

"That's right. Then you'll feel free to enjoy yourself."

While we waited for the storm to pass, we did all the inside cleaning that we could and then played a few games of ping pong. The strong gusts of wind shook the fragile windows. It was *raining cats and dogs.*

"Good game, Alex. You sure have an eye."

"Thanks, for the game, Mom. *What a sport!*"

The storm left as quick as it came. Unlatching the window covers, we looked out over the volleyball court onto the picnic area. "Mother, look at all the moss and branches there are to pick up," Alex observed.

"There you go, Alex, putting that good eye to use again. Why don't you clean up the volleyball court and I'll finish cleaning inside here." Alex grabbed a rake from the closet and a trash can from the corner and proceeded out to the muddy court to clean up the debris. The brisk storm had left the atmosphere cool and crisp.

Looking out the window while I finished tidying up the recreation area I saw Alex swatting at something. "What is it?" I called out. He was swinging the rake trying to shoo something away. He ran up to the grass landing where I was. I swung open the screen door.

"Quick, come inside, take cover in here," I motioned. "Are you alright?" I asked examining his arms for bites.

"Yes, I'm alright. They didn't bite, they just itch, and there are lots of them." The swarming bugs were the little black beetles we had recently noticed around the camp. "Look, there goes another one," I said, moving to avoid contact with the hard-shelled insect.

I discovered that some of the bugs had gotten in through the screens. Over in the corner was a pile of the hard covered beetles. Alex walked over to look at them closer. Bending down he said, "Look at their hard covering; it looks just like a shield. Mom, I remember when I was a little boy, you always told me not to touch insects because they could be dangerous. I will never forget that."

"You remembered!" I cheered. "That's right. Always be careful with insects. Moms are pleased when our children remember what we say."

We closed up the building after we finished our work. *Crunch*, I stepped on one of the hard bugs. "Ooh," I said as another one flew by grazing my forehead.

"You're right, Son, they don't bite, they're just a little irritating." We turned off the lights, locked up, and headed back home.

Protection, care, and refuge were some of the greatest principles the Lord had taught me, and the prayer of a mother's heart is to teach these things to her children. My desire was to direct Alex to understand the care and protection of the Lord.

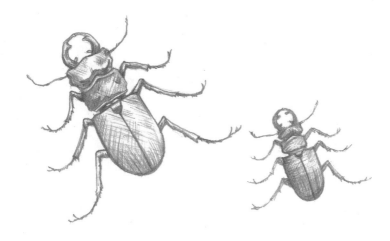

"That's just like the Lord to use nature to teach us His loving ways," I said, thinking about the black beetle we had just encountered.

"How is that Mom?" Alex asked curiously.

"Notice that the black beetle has a hard shell over him to protect his soft body underneath. What a wonderful creation God made!"

"And you came inside to take refuge from the storm." I reminded him.

"I got it, Mom. The hard shell protects the beetle from harm."

"That's right Alex. Sometimes you may feel that God's commandment to honor parents seems difficult. But parents are designed to be the covering over their children to shield them and protect them from harm. Parents do this in obedience to the Lord and because we love our children."

Not only had the storm cleared, but our understanding of God's love and protection seemed clearer to us as well. We began our downhill descent from our busy but heartfelt afternoon.

"Mom, thanks for being my covering and for loving and protecting me."

"With gratitude, I too, humbly accept God's shield and covering over me, Alex."

When the storms of life come our way, we know where to go "under cover."

Beetles have waterproof, shield-like wing cases that protect another more delicate set of hind wings. Beetles eat plants and other insects. Beetles do not live in extremely cold climates. Lightning bugs are also called "luminescent beetles." Beetles are often referred to as the "crunch bug" because of the loud noise their hard shell makes when crushed.

Discussion

Can you explain what it means to be "under cover"? Can you name one way God's Word protects you? How are your parents like a shield over you? How does God protect your family through authority (e.g., police, church, local government)? What are some ways you can show respect to your parents?

Scripture

"The Lord is my strength and my shield; my heart trust in him, and I am helped." Psalm 28:7a

"You have been a refuge for the poor, a refuge for the needy in his distress, a shelter from the storm and a shade from the heat." Isaiah 25:4a

"Finally, be strong in the Lord and in his mighty power. Put on the full armor of God so that you can take your stand against the devil's schemes." Ephesians 6:10–11

Song

"A Mighty Fortress Is Our God" and "Trust And Obey"

Application

Parents, use an umbrella to demonstrate the cover and protection of authority. Plan an evening for catching lightning bugs. Assemble a full set of the Armor of God according to Ephesians 6. Include a belt, breastplate, shoes, shield, helmet, and sword. Keep handy a "rainy-day list" of projects to do on those stormy days. The next time you are caught inside because of poor weather, make a tent out of sheets or blankets and huddle "undercover."

Idiom

Raining cats and dogs refers to a heavy rain.
What a sport means someone who is agreeable.

Prayer

Thank the Lord for protecting you and giving you loving parents.

Chapter 36

Inspector Spritz

"Honor your father and mother"—which is
the first commandment with a promise."

EPHESIANS 6:2

It was early in the evening, almost twilight. The summer was full blown. Warm winds stirred up the dust and pollen as well as our desires for outdoor adventures. Anticipation was in the air around the camp. The season's wildlife was actively delivering litters of raccoons, squirrels, and birds of prey.

"Mom, can I go down to the pond and throw my line in for a little while? The fish ought to be biting by now." The longer days and absence of schoolwork allowed time for extra evening activities.

"Yes, and be sure to take your flashlight. *Better safe than sorry.* Darkness sneaks up on you before you know it, and who knows what you'll run into out here in the country."

"Okay, thanks, Mom. I'll come straight home before dark."

"Bye, love you. Hope you catch a big one!" I ushered him out the door with a blessing. Alex fled to the shed to get his fishing gear.

We loved living high on a hill. We could watch from afar as fishermen of all sorts threw their poles in the fishing hole. Alex was the only one out tonight, and watching for him to pull in his big catch was a mother's treat. The sun disappeared over the horizon bringing welcome relief from its rays.

From my window look-out, I caught a glimpse of Alex's white t-shirt. He stood perfectly still so as not to alert the fish of his presence. *The fish must not be biting tonight,* I thought. It was getting darker, and thinking Alex would be coming home soon, I started cleaning up the supper dishes and soon lost track of time. The clock ticked away, and when I looked up, it was completely dark.

He should be back by now, I thought. I was not panicked. The camp was perfectly safe, and he had been in clear view from the house. Peering out the window, I could not see the white t-shirt, or much of anything else even though the moon was on the rise. *He must be at the recreation room,* I thought. It was not uncommon to find a small group gathered for a game of foosball or tetherball on these hot summer nights. So, I jumped in the car to go find Alex. I was not concerned, just aware of the time.

Driving on the hill near the cabins, I turned on my bright lights looking for the white t-shirt. Shining my state-of-the-art, dazzling flashlight that we called "Torch" out the window, I caught a glimpse of Rick, the maintenance man, finishing some evening work.

"Rick, have you seen Alex tonight?" In our small community, we watched over one another.

"Yes, I saw him just about fifteen minutes ago walking around the pond toward the burn pile. He had his fishing pole with him."

"Oh, okay, he must have gone to dig for worms. Thanks, Rick, I'll catch up with him. See you later." The burn pile was on the way home, so I figured Alex was headed in the right direction. There was no further need for me to continue looking for him; he would be home soon.

The moon was high and bright, and the critters were out in numbers. Glancing out my bedroom window, I could see the moon reflecting on the road that curved around in front of our house. Still, there was no Alex. I was picking up around the house, preparing to call it a night, when I heard the back door close.

I smelled him before I saw him. "Alex, is that you?"

In a low whisper, he answered, "Yes, Ma'am." A thud followed his words, and the floorboards creaked. I went into the kitchen and flipped on the light. There was Alex with a long look on his face. His tackle box was plopped down beside him—the cause of the thud.

"Alex, you got spritzed!"

"Just a little."

"It smells like he got you big time!" The stench quickly permeated through the house. I winced but felt relieved that he was home safe and sound. His eyes were glazed over like a sleep-walker.

"Why don't you go wash up, and then you can tell me what happened." After sponging down in tomato juice, bathing and changing his clothes, Alex continued his story.

"I ran into trouble on the way back from the pond," he explained.

"Trouble? What do you mean?" I was anxious to hear the whole story.

"The fish weren't biting, so I went digging for worms. Then I heard something moving in an old, rotten log." His lips quivered as he spoke.

"What happened next?" I listened intently.

"I heard the leaves rustling," he continued. "When I moved to take a closer look, there was a loud hiss, and before I knew it, I was face to tail with a skunk. Mom, I was flabbergasted! I thought it was a cat. I tore out of there as fast as I could, but he still got me."

"You couldn't tell what it was with your flashlight?"

"Well, actually, Mom, I didn't take my flashlight with me this time. I thought just this one time I didn't need it. I thought I'd be home before dark. It's a good thing he didn't spray me more than he did."

"Why, you smell like he doused you from head to toe, Inspector Spritz! Looks like leaving your flashlight at home got you just a little spritzed. Sin works the same way, Alex. A little spritz, a lot of spritz, it all stinks the same. And, that's the *gist of it*—next time, obey in the small things, too!"

"Yes, and it'll be a long time before I go around inspecting logs or anything else in the dark. And next time, I'll come straight home like I told you. God showed me through this that I need to honor you at all times."

"That's a great idea, Alex. Let's commit this smelly lesson to memory with a glass of tomato juice." We raised our glasses together. "And now for a toast: Three cheers to no stinky sins!"

> *Skunks' defense is so effective that it is seldom attacked. First-time, naive predators quickly learn to avoid skunks. The primary predator of the skunk is the great horned owl. Spritz is another word for spray. Skunks will also hiss and whine when they are scared. Skunks can carry rabies which can make them unpredictable. NEVER approach a wild animal, especially a skunk.*

Discussion

How would taking a flashlight have made a difference in this story? What is the analogy between a flashlight and God's Word? How does obeying your parents demonstrate honor to them and to God? Why is it so important to obey in small things as well as big things?

Scripture

"Your word is a lamp to my feet and a light for my path." Psalm 119:105

"Whoever can be trusted with very little can also be trusted with much, and whoever is dishonest with very little will also be dishonest with much." Luke 16:10

"This is love for God: to obey his commands. And his commands are not burdensome." 1 John 5:3

Song

"This Little Light of Mine" and "Praise God From Whom All Blessings Flow"

Activity

On a sunny day, have a water balloon or squirt gun party, and remember Inspector Spritz.

Application

Shine a flashlight against the wall and make shadow puppets. Be creative, and act out a skit with your puppets. Memorize Ephesians 6:2. Craft a plaque of the phrase: "Blessings Follow Obedience." Place it in a central location as a reminder. Pick a night to serve tomato juice, with a "cheers" to no stinky sins!

Idiom

Gist of it means the main point of something.
Better safe than sorry means caution can prevent problems later.

Prayer

Pray and ask the Lord to help you honor your Mother and Father. Thank Him for the blessings that come from obedience.

Topic Index

*By wisdom a house is built, and through
understanding it is established;*

Proverbs 24:3

A Special Note

My first memory of hearing about Jesus was at a backyard Bible School. A faithful servant of the Lord came weekly and shared the Bible with the children of that neighborhood. I am eternally grateful for the love and devotion to Christ that this precious lady demonstrated. Her sowing of God's Word on those warm summer mornings is responsible for me hearing the Good News of Jesus Christ.

It is my desire to illustrate the impact that a small gathering like backyard Bible School can leave on a young child's heart and mind. The Lord used these simple exposures to the Word of God to draw me to Himself. There are eternal rewards for those who take the time to plant seeds of God's Word in the lives of His little children.

Scripture

"Jesus answered, 'I am the way and the truth and the life. No one comes to the Father except through me.'" John 14:6

"In the past God overlooked such ignorance, but now he commands all people everywhere to repent. For he has set a day when he will judge the world with justice by the man he has appointed. He has given proof of this to all men by raising him from the dead." Acts 17: 30–31

"That if you confess with your mouth, 'Jesus is Lord,' and believe in your heart that God raised him from the dead, you will be saved. For it is with your heart that you believe and are justified, and it is with your mouth that you confess and are saved." Romans 10:9–10

"For it is by grace you have been saved, through faith—and this not from yourselves, it is the gift of God—not by works, so that no one can boast." Ephesians 2:8–9

Benediction: From the Author

May my simple remembrances of days gone by and lessons learned from the providence of our Great Teacher inspire you to write down what God has done in your life with your children. May these be the patterns of faith to follow for generations to come, fulfilling the admonition of Deuteronomy 11:18–19:

"Fix these words of mine in your hearts and minds; tie them as symbols on your hands and bind them on your foreheads. Teach them to your children, talking about them when you sit at home and when you walk along the road, when you lie down and when you get up."

Alex and Lynn Marie

2002, San Antonio, Texas

Biography

Lynn Marie Hurtado was born and raised in Florida. Her devotion to the Word of God has led her to be involved in missions for the past thirteen years. She is currently a curriculum developer and an international ESL instructor for Asian English students of all ages. Lynn Marie homeschooled her son Alex for eleven years. With this experience, Lynn Marie has a passion for encouraging other parents to invest in their children's future, spiritual lives, and education. Lynn Marie currently lives in South Texas.

Homeschooling afforded Alex many opportunities to be involved with missions at a young age. These unique educational experiences influenced his desire to pursue a career in law enforcement. He is presently employed with a law enforcement agency while pursuing various certifications relating to this field. Alex still has a passion for spending time in the great outdoors where he lives in the Texas Hill Country.

Lynn Marie can be contacted at: LynnMarie@SkunkTalesOnline.com

Do You Have a
Skunk Tale?

Do you have an inspiring or uplifting tale to tell? We invite you to contribute a story for a future edition of Skunk Tales. Please share your story with us of how God brought you through an original or unique circumstance. Your testimony could teach, encourage, and inspire future readers.

For more information on how to submit your Skunk Tales, visit:

Skunktalesonline.com

To mail your Skunk Tales, please send them to this address:

New Lineage
P.O. Box 293892
Kerrville, Texas 78029

We would love to hear how the stories you read in this book have affected you and which ones are your favorites.

Blessings,

Lynn Marie Hurtado

Write Your Skunk Tale